Happily Remarried

DAVID & LISA FRISBIE

HARVEST HOUSE PUBLISHERS
EUGENE, OREGON

All Scripture quotations are taken from the Good News Translation—Second Edition © 1992 by American Bible Society. Used by permission.

Cover by Koechel Peterson & Associates, Inc., Minneapolis, Minnesota

Cover photo © Thinkstock/Getty Images

Statement About Privacy and Identification

Persons and couples appear in this book in one of two ways:

Where persons or couples are mentioned using *both* first and last names, these persons or couples are either public figures or have consented in writing that we may tell their stories, identifying them, quoting them by name, or both. We are grateful to those who have not only told us their stories but have also allowed us to identify them.

Where persons or couples are mentioned using first names only, certain key details of the story (including but not limited to names, location, marital status, and number and gender of children) have been altered to prevent identification of the subjects while retaining the integrity of the narrative. We have found that remarried couples, perhaps even more so than other families, highly value their privacy and their anonymity. With regard to first-name-only stories, any resemblance to any person of the same name, or in the same location, or in a similar situation, is therefore entirely coincidental.

HAPPILY REMARRIED
Copyright © 2005 by David and Lisa Frisbie
Published by Harvest House Publishers
Eugene, Oregon 97402

Library of Congress Cataloging-in-Publication Data
Frisbie, David, 1955–
Happily remarried / David and Lisa Frisbie.
p. cm.
ISBN-13: 978-0-7369-1530-4
ISBN-10: 0-7369-1530-3 (pbk.)
1. Remarried people—Religious life. 2. Remarriage—Religious aspects—Christianity.
I. Frisbie, Lisa, 1956- II. Title.
BV4596.R45F75 2005
248.8'44—dc22   2005001514

Printed in the United States of America

05   06   07   08   09   10   11   12   / VP-CF /   10   9   8   7   6   5   4   3   2

To Rev. Ray and Wilma Bridges of Chattanooga, Tennessee, who pastored churches throughout the southeastern United States. Romance sparkled in their happy marriage through 76 years of committed union. With sturdy optimism and unfailing good humor, they faced all their challenges together, side by side, a shining example of loving togetherness.

And to Arthur and Mattie Uphaus of Spring Hill, Kansas. Arthur worked the land for much of his life. Mattie was a writer and college professor. This long-term married couple modeled romance in marriage and exemplified serving each other in love. Eyes twinkling, their smiles lit up the lives of all those around them. Mattie, now a widow, remains an inspiration and role model for both of us. She is one of our greatest encouragers.

And with hearts full of gratitude, to our parents: Ruth and Lamont Jacobson of Minneapolis, and Lee and Marilyn Frisbie of Kansas City. At this writing Ruth and Lamont are celebrating 56 happy years together; Lee and Marilyn are celebrating 54 years of joyous marriage. Both these couples have lived out exemplary relationships before us. They continue to inspire us with their loving examples of committed, godly union.

Acknowledgments

We are indebted to Clinton and Emily Crowder of Baltimore, Maryland, who are friends of the heart. Through Emily's friendship with Elizabeth Atcheson we learned of the existence of the Jerry B. Jenkins Christian Writers Guild and its conferences for Christian speakers and authors. We owe the existence of this book to our friendship with Emily and Clinton, and thus also to Jerry Jenkins, Wayne Atcheson, and their dedicated staff at CWG.

It was Terry Glaspey of Harvest House Publishers who first believed in this project, and who first suggested that the lessons and experiences we had gleaned from working with remarried couples might well serve other remarriages through the ministry of publication. Terry is greatly gifted as a speaker and author and is one of the most gracious Christian gentlemen we have ever known. Our debt to him is incalculable.

As other authors have discovered before us, the editorial, marketing, and support team at Harvest House Publishers of Eugene, Oregon, is a talented group of people who are absolutely committed to serving God through publishing. We have been blessed by the insight, commitment, and expertise of the entire Harvest House publishing family. Our deepest gratitude to all of you!

A word of thanks is due to the more than 300 couples who have invited us to conduct and perform all or part of their wedding ceremonies. In many cases, this invitation involved us in four to six sessions of premarital counseling with the bridal couples. We've learned as much or more from these sessions as we have from the universities and graduate schools we've attended.

Traveling to speak at marriage conferences, camps, retreats, and seminars has continued our education. We learned more from listening than from speaking; more from hearing the stories of others than from telling our own. We owe a debt of gratitude to all who have shared with us along our journey.

And to the many remarried couples who have opened their stories to us, especially those with children being blended into new family units, thanks for your courage, your honesty, and your willingness to share your wisdom with us and with our readers. This book is not about us or our experiences. It is about you: your setbacks and challenges, but also your successes and achievements.

In all these pages, may God be glorified! May the words in this book help to accomplish God's divine purposes in all of us, especially as we serve in and honor our primary roles as husbands, wives, and parents of growing children.

CONTENTS

Light for Your Journey

N THE HISTORY OF THE UNIVERSE, there has been only one perfect person.

He remained single all his life and died young.

The rest of us are imperfect creatures, deeply flawed, struggling to find our way through the complex maze of relationships and choices we encounter. We make mistakes, we learn and grow, we adapt and move on.

Some of us do our learning at an early age, growing by trial and error. Some of us make our discoveries much later in life, almost by chance it seems. Many of us are somewhere in between, in the "middle ages," wondering why we aren't smarter or more successful or somehow better at all of this.

If you have experienced the end of a marriage and find yourself beginning again in a new relationship, this book is for you. If you are now married to a person who has prior marriage experience, this book is for you.

This is a book about forgiveness and grace, about courage and hope, about exploring new ways to build a lasting marriage and a lifelong love.

There are some helpful ideas here, some starting places. There are some stories of people who are making it work, even though it's not easy.

In these few chapters, may you encounter reasons to believe and to trust.

If there is light for your journey here, may it shine clearly on all your pathways.

CHAPTER ONE

The Journey Begins

✦

*J*OANIE IS GETTING married today.

Less than three hours before the ceremony, she's receiving a final fitting on her wedding dress. She tugs at her hemline, smoothing an imaginary wrinkle.

"How do I look?" she asks daughter Ashley, age 11.

"You look great, Mom!" Ashley exclaims, smiling.

Joanie is not convinced.

"I look fat," she frowns, checking her reflection in a trifold mirror.

Two friends, helping her prepare for the big event, tell her otherwise.

She stares intently into the mirror.

"I look old, too," she insists.

Thirty years old and busy raising her pre-teen daughter, Joanie is getting married for the first time. More than anything else, she's excited for Ashley, who will finally be gaining a father figure around the house.

Joanie brushes her hair, still frowning.

"I just want everything to be perfect today," she says with a sigh.

Things were not so perfect a dozen years ago, when Joanie told her churchgoing parents about the pregnancy. Barely out of high school, she was living at home, attending community college, and working a part-time job.

The pregnancy shocked and disappointed her family.

"They were so upset," Joanie remembers. "I didn't even tell them until I was almost five months along. By then, I was already starting to show."

Her parents were traumatized. How could a young Christian woman, raised in a caring and healthy church and home, get pregnant?

The baby's father was a young man on the fringes of the church, the son of divorced parents who lived in another state. "I'm not going to marry you just because you got pregnant," he told Joanie. "It's your mess, so you can decide what you want to do."

Abortion was out of the question in Joanie's mind. She kept the baby, remained in her parents' home for a while, and kept going to the same church.

"Some of my parents' friends were incredibly sweet to me," she says. "They gave me a really nice baby shower, offered to help in any way they could, and just went out of their way to show me what love is all about."

There were other kinds of people in the church too—and not all of Joanie's experiences in the congregation were positive and encouraging.

More than a decade later, Joanie can hardly talk about some of the comments she heard, directly and otherwise, from well-intentioned church people. She's tried to forgive them, just as she hopes they've forgiven her by now.

Meanwhile, eleven years and four months after Ashley's birth, Joanie is finally getting married for the first time. She's excited about that, but also afraid. She worries about the transition she and Ashley will be making: from just the two of them at home, to sharing their space with three males.

MARK, JOANIE'S HUSBAND-TO-BE, isn't worried about it at all.

"Joanie's great with my two sons," he beams. "She's so good at all those things a woman does better than a man. I've watched my boys react to her, and it's obvious they already love her a lot!"

Mark, 42 years old and divorced, was awarded primary custody of sons Caleb, 14, and Joshua, 12. Mark's wife left him for another man, moving across the country to begin an entirely new life.

Their divorce has been final for two years.

"It's been lonely without a woman around the house," Mark admits a few hours before the ceremony. "And when you're 40 years old, dating is just weird! God brought Joanie into my life at the perfect time. I'm ready to settle down and be a normal family again, like it should be."

"Joanie's really nice," Joshua agrees while trying on his wedding tuxedo. "But she's not my real mom. My mom lives in California now."

"She lives in Mendocino," Caleb adds.

Clad in matching gray tuxes, Mark and his sons make their way through the Mall of America toward a small chapel at the edge of its southeast corner. As they arrive, they notice that a previous service is just ending.

"I guess we're a little early, guys," Mark tells his sons.

The three men linger in a sunny atrium, waiting for Joanie and Ashley. Josh and Caleb take turns riding escalators first up, then back down, always staying within sight of their father.

"They're gonna love having a woman in the house again," Mark confides to a friend who arrives early also. "I mean, I've sorta learned how to cook and all, but it's just not the same when a guy is cooking and cleaning and doing all those household things, ya know?"

The friend nods in agreement. "You're a lucky guy," he tells Mark. "Joanie is really nice, and her daughter is just the same. Both of them are total sweethearts!"

"You'll become the new Brady Bunch," another arriving friend chimes in. It's not the first time Mark has heard the comparison, but he laughs politely.

Joshua spies his new sister far across the mall. "They're coming, Dad!" he calls excitedly from a downward escalator.

Mark smiles and waves in reply. "Thanks, bud!" he yells.

Within minutes, Joanie, Ashley, and two of Joanie's friends arrive at the entrance to the small chapel. Caleb and Joshua return from riding the escalators. Mark introduces his friends to Joanie's friends as the wedding photographer also arrives.

"How about some quick candid shots, since we've got time?" the photographer offers. Reaching into a bulging bag, he extracts a digital camera. "Just ignore me," he advises. "Go ahead and talk."

Trying to act natural, the wedding party attempts to make small talk. The effort fails, to everyone's amusement.

Mark, outgoing and confident, begins to make exaggerated gestures as he speaks, mugging for the camera. The photographer chuckles loudly, and everyone laughs and relaxes.

Laughter and photographs are still going on as the collar-clad minister steps out of the chapel and into the mall walkway. "We're ready for you now," he announces, opening the door of the chapel and motioning everyone inside. The group moves, en masse, through the chapel's entrance.

As they wait for other guests, the bride and groom review the order of service for their wedding ceremony.

Ashley will be at her mother's side, serving as the maid of honor.

Josh and Caleb will both be groomsmen, each one equally a

"best man." There are no other attendants. Both Mark and Joanie have insisted on simplicity. There has been no rehearsal and thus no rehearsal dinner, saving time and money for everyone involved.

This wedding, like those in many second marriages, has a tight budget. Every effort has been made to have a nice ceremony but keep expenses low.

The invited guests are few. Mark's parents, who have been supportive of this union and who adore Ashley, are paying for the chapel and for the minister. Joanie's parents, who have warmed to Mark gradually over time, are paying for a celebration dinner after the ceremony.

Mark has invited half-a-dozen friends from church and work; Joanie has done the same. Each friend was allowed to bring one guest, and only one guest.

Rounding out the small crowd are friends of the children: Each child could invite one guest. Ashley has invited her best friend from church; Josh and Caleb have each included a close friend from school.

The schedule is not extensive. After a brief welcome, the couple will exchange vows and rings. There will be no singing, no candles, and no mention of Mark's prior marriage. Mark's ex-wife was not invited to the service.

Ashley's father has not stayed in contact with Joanie. He has not paid, and Joanie has not pursued, any form of child support across the years.

INCLUDING THE MINISTER, the organist, and a receptionist in the chapel office, there are 29 people at Mark and Joanie's wedding on this Saturday afternoon.

The bride and groom, smiling, greet each guest at the back of the chapel.

Standing nearby, the minister beckons to the bridal couple. It's nearly time for the brief ceremony to begin.

"Does everyone know their places?" the minister inquires.

"Yes," Mark assures him. "We just reviewed all that at lunchtime."

"Well then, let's roll," the clergyman says with a smile.

The organist starts a medley of contemporary Christian worship songs. Guests quit talking and take their seats. With no ushers, there is little formality. Ashley, standing beside her mom, looks around the room for her young friend, who, it turns out, is pointing a disposable camera at the two women.

Josh and Caleb's friends are missing. Both are shooting baskets at a sporting-goods store on the far side of the mall. They arrive at the last moment.

Exactly on time, the organist booms out the wedding march.

Joanie and Ashley walk together, hand-in-hand, up the center aisle.

Cameras flash as Mark, Caleb, and Joshua receive the women at the front of the chapel. All five members of the newly formed family stand side by side, facing the minister, their backs to the assembled crowd.

Mark's father checks the volume on his video camera.

The minister gives a word of welcome, then prays a short prayer. In a brief homily, he speaks of accepting each other, making compromises as needed, and staying committed for the long term. His tone is light but meaningful. He attempts a few jokes, which succeed.

Vows are recited without error.

On cue, Ashley hands Mark's ring to Joanie. Caleb hands Joanie's ring to Mark. In a previously arranged surprise, Joshua passes a handmade necklace to his father. It's for the bride, who is teary-eyed as she receives it.

Rings installed, necklace latched, the bridal couple clasp hands.

The minister pronounces the couple legally married, and applause breaks out from the audience. Mark and Joanie exchange a kiss as their children watch.

Twenty minutes after the organist's first note, the wedding is over.

The minister hands Mark two signed copies of the marriage license. "It's official! Congratulations!"

"That was a very nice service, Reverend," Mark responds.

"When do we eat?" booms a voice from the back of the room.

Everyone laughs.

"Does anyone need a map?" Mark asks his guests. "I've got maps right here. It's really easy to find—just head straight south on Cedar."

An upscale grocery store nearby features a restaurant on its premises. The wedding party has reserved four tables in a corner. Conveniently, the grocer has also furnished the wedding cake: chocolate with white frosting.

Twenty-four people (the staff at the chapel were invited, but declined; one couple from Joanie's work pleaded a prior commitment) successfully arrive. They make their way through the store to the dining area.

Beautifully wrapped wedding gifts are carried in, although the invitations very deliberately announced "No Gifts, Please!" Everyone, it seems, has totally ignored that announcement. The gifts are practical but generous: a new DVD player for the whole family, a large tent for camping, five movie passes to a local theater chain. Everyone has given with the family in mind.

Gifts are opened, orders are taken, cake is sliced, and happy laughter echoes around the tables. The kids have a table of their own.

Two hours later, the last goodbyes are being said. Guests help carry the wedding presents and clear the clutter off the tables. Joanie's father leaves a very generous tip as he pays the tab.

During the party, the sun has set—it's Saturday evening.

Caleb, Joshua, and Ashley will be spending the weekend with Mark's parents. The boys have stayed with these grandparents frequently, and love them. The grandparents, for their part, are delighted to have a granddaughter in the mix.

With the kids well cared-for, Mark and Joanie have reserved a suite at the Nicollet Island Inn, a romantic hotel along the river in downtown Minneapolis. For their honeymoon, the bridal couple will enjoy two nights at the hotel, strolling to shops along the riverfront in brisk, beautiful fall weather.

With the Minnesota Vikings in town for a home game—and since Mark is a major sports fan—the newlyweds will see a game at the Metrodome on Sunday.

"How's that for being romantic?" Joanie laughs.

"Hey, the seats are *together!*" Mark insists.

The couple waves goodbye to their kids as grandpa's giant SUV makes its way slowly out of the crowded parking lot.

"Well, it's finally just you and me, babe!" Mark beams at his bride. Joanie smiles and kisses him, lingering a bit.

STROLLING HAND IN HAND to their pickup truck, the newlyweds are unaware that roughly 60 percent of remarriages eventually end in divorce. According to the experts, being involved in a prior marriage actually decreases the odds of a second marriage becoming permanent and enduring.

None of this matters to Mark and Joanie on the crisp autumn day they're beginning their brief honeymoon. They are in love. They're delighted to be forming a new family. Their future seems bright and unclouded.

"I really think we're going to make it," Joanie has told a friend during the happy reception. "Mark is such a caring man, his sons are so well-behaved, and Ashley finally has a daddy in the house. It's going to be perfect!"

"Joanie is so different from my ex-wife," Mark has quietly told a friend. "She's everything my ex is not: sweet, tender, and positive. I really think this marriage is going to be different for me. This one is going to last!"

Will Mark and Joanie beat the odds? Will their marriage

grow and thrive amid the challenges of blending a family and setting up a new household?

In the chapters that follow, we'll look at the four "first principles" of helping a second marriage succeed. We'll take an honest look at the problems blended families can expect to encounter. We'll learn from the examples of others who have traveled this road before, and who talk openly about their experiences. And, finally, we'll go through some questions that will give you a chance to think over or talk over the issues we've raised.

Join us in these pages as we explore "a second chance at forever."

Part One

The Four
"First Principles"
for Building a
Strong Second Marriage

CHAPTER TWO

Principle Number One

Form a Spiritual Connection Centered on Serving God

*God has already placed Jesus Christ
as the one and only foundation,
and no other foundation can be laid.*

1 CORINTHIANS 3:11

*P*AULA ISN'T OPEN TO ANYTHING that sounds religious.

"This isn't a spiritual problem," she insists. "This is a relationship issue. I know we both need to pay more attention to God, but that's not why I'm here. I'm here because the relationship just isn't working!"

Paula is frustrated and looking for answers. From her perspective, it makes no sense to talk about spirituality when the problem seems social and relational. As she sees things, a person's spiritual life is a separate category, something that really doesn't intersect with other parts of his or her existence. She just wants help with her marriage; what does spiritual growth have to do with that?

Do you separate your life into categories like Paula does?

As we work with couples considering remarriage, there are a number of questions we typically ask. The first of these questions centers on the spiritual aspect of the previous marriage.

21

This is the question that surprises Paula.

"What does spirituality have to do with marriage issues?" Paula inquires. "And why are you asking about my spirituality in the prior relationship?"

We humans are complicated creatures, composed of many separate parts that are connected and interrelated in mysterious ways. Dividing our experience into segments misses the big picture: that we are whole persons, constantly growing and changing. Each area of our lives impacts each other area: each part influences the whole.

Whether she realizes it or not, Paula's emotional life can definitely affect her level of physical health. Whether she has considered it or not, Paula's spiritual life (or the absence of one) may be a factor in whether her new marriage is thriving and growing, or whether it is falling back into old, unhelpful patterns. For Paula, this is an entirely new concept.

The Single Most Important Thing

Here's a relevant question we raise in many different venues: *"What is the single most important thing you can do to guard and protect your second marriage, giving it hope to succeed and thrive?"*

We ask this question of remarried couples and those about to remarry.

We rarely get a response that centers in spirituality. God doesn't get mentioned; people tend to think in terms of behaviors or attitudes instead.

Typically, we receive answers like "have a lot of forgiveness" or maybe "just start fresh" or perhaps "dedicate yourself to trying harder this time."

These are wonderful answers, but they miss the main point.

We have found that the single most important thing you can do to guard and protect your second marriage is to deliberately focus it on serving God. When both partners commit themselves to keeping God first, positive things begin to happen in every other aspect of the marriage relationship.

Does this mean that God, or religion, is some kind of magic cure for all relational difficulties? Of course not. Yet in this chapter we'll discover ways in which centering a marriage on God changes husbands and wives for the better.

Psychologists studying marital fulfillment are discovering a significant correlation between religious activity and marital longevity. Similarly, we are noticing a strong link between religious activity and happiness in marriage.

Simply put, "religiously active" persons are more likely to remain in a committed relationship—and they are also more likely to label themselves as "happy" within the context of that committed relationship.

"Serious About God"

Here's another question we use. We ask remarried couples to reflect on their previous experience of marriage by responding to this: "Thinking about your previous experience of marriage, would you say that both partners, only one of you, or neither of you were serious about God?"

Our question makes no effort to define "serious about God" and allows each respondent to make a personal judgment about what "serious" means.

What we hear is very enlightening. As couples think about their previous marriages, only 13 percent of those we surveyed describe a relationship in which both persons were serious about God. Occasion-

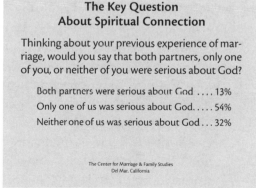

The Key Question About Spiritual Connection

Thinking about your previous experience of marriage, would you say that both partners, only one of you, or neither of you were serious about God?

Both partners were serious about God 13%
Only one of us was serious about God..... 54%
Neither one of us was serious about God ... 32%

The Center for Marriage & Family Studies
Del Mar, California

ally, in verbal feedback after the question, it appears the percentage may be even lower.

"Well, I *thought* we were both serious about God," Janet tells us after answering that both partners were serious. "But when Darren left me, he quit attending church. I had to really hassle him to get him to take the kids to church when they stayed with him on weekends. So was he really serious about God, or was he just going along with what I wanted during our time together?"

Karen echoes this same theme. "Once Mike and I were divorced, I noticed he quit doing anything public about his religious beliefs. He quit going to church. He didn't participate in any kind of organized Bible study or men's group. If he honestly believed in God, it sure didn't show in the choices he made with his time.

"Looking back, I now realize I was usually the one pushing us to go to church, to get to know people at church, to go to retreats, and so on. Since Mike always went along with me, I assumed that our beliefs and values were about the same. I *thought* we were both serious about God. We went to church all the time, and we gave money to the church fairly regularly. Isn't that serious?"

Karen's original answer puts her among the 13 percent, but in follow-up talks she raises the same kind of issues that Janet does. Although it seemed like both partners were serious about God at the time, was that really the case?

If you have previous experience with marriage, how would *you* answer the question about your prior relationship? Were both of you serious about God, or was one of you usually doing more "pushing" toward religious activities? If only one of you was serious, which one was it: you or your partner?

Janet says more about her former marriage.

"All my life, I had been looking for a spiritual leader," she said. "When I got married, I wanted my husband to be the clear spiritual leader of our family. I hoped our kids would have a dad who was an excellent example for them.

"Darren went to church with me, but I never saw him praying or reading the Bible or doing anything religious around the house. Still, I kept hoping that somehow he'd still become the spiritual leader I always dreamed of marrying.

"When he left me, I was completely devastated. I hadn't seen it coming. But looking back, I wonder…was his lack of interest in spiritual things a sign that maybe other areas of his life were coming unglued?"

Take Time to Pray Together

How do remarried couples come together in the first place? Usually there is a strong common interest or a shared experience. Perhaps both persons are single parents, struggling with the issues of child-raising, financial stress, and managing a busy household. A bond emerges and grows, and out of the bonding, affection begins.

A relationship centered on affection will last as long as the affection does. Building a relationship around a common interest can help attachment to grow and develop, yet many couples stop building the relationship as soon as they say "we do." Unless they work at it intentionally, even a happy and loving couple can end up traveling in separate directions, pursuing separate goals and values.

Forming a spiritual connection that centers on God is the single most important priority for building a lasting marriage. And among all the methods of forming a meaningful spiritual connection, the most valuable is prayer.

"My prayer life is personal," Melissa insists. "I'm not sure I could feel comfortable sharing it with another person."

Do you share Melissa's feelings about prayer? If so, you may miss one of the most effective bonding experiences that's available to married couples. To paraphrase the truism, the couple that prays together, stays together.

How does this work in real life?

Gary is a morning person; Linda rises as late as possible. Yet the two of them have discovered the power of praying together.

Here's how they do it: Every evening at a fixed time, they go to a room in their home, close the door, and spend a half-hour or so praying together. They do this on good days, bad days, sick days, stressful days, and every other kind of day also.

Admits Linda, "It was incredibly hard to get started with this. First of all, we hadn't seen a model of praying together in any other couple. None of our friends were actively doing anything like this.

"Secondly, we couldn't find a time that was good for both of us. Gary loves the early mornings and is really focused at that time of day. He was gung-ho to partner with me in prayer in the early morning—but my brain doesn't even function until noon, if then.

"When we finally settled on praying together in the evenings, it seemed like everything kind of conspired against the time we had chosen. The phone would ring. The kids would need us. There were interruptions and setbacks almost every night.

"Finally, we just decided that at 9 PM, we were going to go into Gary's study, close the door, flip the phone over to the answering machine, and pray. Our youngest daughter goes to bed at 8:30; the older two were instructed not to bother us unless the house was on fire."

Linda pauses to make sure we're listening.

"And you know what? The house hasn't burned down. It's like once we decided to make prayer an absolute priority, then everything else kind of yielded to that. These days, it's very rare to have an interruption."

Gary adds his perspective. "I'm tired by 9 PM," he admits. "Some nights I really don't feel like praying, and I especially don't feel like praying out loud. I'm just too tired. But the truth is, the nights I feel like skipping prayer always turn out to be our best times together, the times that feel most powerful, most effective, and most meaningful as we pray. I'm learning to watch for tiredness as a signal that we're about to have a powerful time together."

Linda agrees. "Now that we're doing this so regularly, I can't imagine giving up this time for anything else. This is one of the best times of our day, a time for just the two of us to be together, to pray for each other, and to come away spiritually and emotionally refreshed and renewed."

"Now that we're doing it, I wouldn't quit for anything," Gary adds.

Sharing the Load, Taking Things to God

Praying together is a powerful unifying activity for married couples. If the idea of praying together for half an hour seems intimidating, start with 10 minutes. The important thing is to make it a priority, establish a regular time, then begin to build a pattern of deliberately, intentionally praying together.

At first, spending even 10 minutes in prayer will seem like an eternity. You may find yourself saying 30-second prayers for each of the kids, followed by 30-second prayers for each other, while glancing at your watch frequently. You'll finish your prayers in less than 10 minutes, then find yourself wondering, *Now what do we do?*

Keep on practicing in prayer. Soon, 10 minutes will stretch into 15 or 20. What once were 30-second prayers for the children will become several minutes in length, and will become much more heartfelt and deep.

Jot prayer needs on a church bulletin or piece of paper, then carry the notes with you into your prayer time later that day. Reminding yourself of things to pray about, especially by writing a note, is an effective tool for growing in prayer.

If one of you is more verbal, it may be that one of you typically prays a lot longer than the other in your shared time. There's nothing wrong with that. The point is that you're together, you're praying, you're sharing the load of marriage and parenting, and you're taking your needs and your issues directly to God.

Sharing in prayer, even if it feels "clunky" at first, is the most effective way to form a lasting spiritual connection with your partner. As you do this, you'll also be forming a lasting spiritual connection with your heavenly Father.

Take Time to Learn Together

Bob and Rachel met at a growth group in their large suburban church.

"It wasn't a singles group," insists Bob. "I wasn't ready to think of myself that way, even though I'd been divorced for almost five years. I had stayed away from the singles scene, even though our church has a great singles ministry."

The two of them were among a dozen or so people in a group that met weekly to talk about the previous Sunday's sermon and pray for each other.

"When Rachel would bring up a prayer request, and talk about what she going through, I could totally relate," Bob tells us. "It was like the challenges she was facing were exactly the ones I was facing."

At first, the two didn't even realize they were attracted to each other. Instead, they became connected as absentee prayer partners, each one praying a lot for the other during the course of an average week.

"We were supposed to pray for everyone in the group," Rachel admits, "and I guess I mostly did that. But when I was praying for Bob, it was so much easier to pray because I could totally relate to his situation with trying to manage the household as a single parent."

"It was the same for me," Bob says. "My prayers for Rachel would always be more extended, and more deep, than my prayers for others in the group. I guess God gave me compassion for what she was going through, even before He gave me compassion for her as a person."

When they began to realize they might have feelings for each other, the couple raised the issue with their small group. To their surprise, the group members were hugely supportive of the potential match.

"I've been praying that you two would find each other!" one woman said. "And my husband has joined me in that prayer."

"I guess everybody else figured it out before we did," Bob laughs. "Once we started getting together socially and involving our kids, everything just kind of 'clicked' between us."

"People were praying for us," Rachel adds. "And just knowing that made everything so much easier than it might have been. For one thing, our kids really liked each other, and we had no idea whether that would happen or not!"

Once they were married, was it hard to continue going to a group?

"Absolutely not," Bob proclaims. "How could we not believe in the power of small groups, when that's what brought us together? This year, for the first time, we're actually serving as devotional leaders for a group."

Rachel smiles. "We work on the devotionals together, although Bob is usually the one doing the talking during group time. We have as much fun getting ready for group as we have during the session itself. Being leaders has really brought us a lot closer to God, and a lot closer to each other."

Taking time to learn together—studying a book of the Bible, a sermon, or a quality Christian bestseller—helps couples connect with each other and grow. Being together in a small group is particularly helpful. At the small-group level, people relax and feel more comfortable making friends and getting acquainted. Meanwhile, broader spiritual purposes such as learning and growth are more easily accomplished.

For a couple in the early stages of a remarriage, few things are as helpful as being surrounded by a caring, praying, supportive network of godly friends. Getting involved in a small group through your local church is one of the simplest and most effective ways to build friendships and find the help you need.

Take Time to Serve Together

Richard is the original missions-trip guy. Married only briefly as a younger man, he has participated in more than a dozen overseas mission trips, working on construction projects for schools, churches, parsonages, and even a hospital ward.

"You name it, I've helped build it," he says, smiling.

Grace, never before married, knew about Richard's high involvement in missions but didn't plan to take it personally after she became his second wife. "I just assumed he'd be gone for a week or so every year, doing some kind of worthy project in a far-away place." She grins. "In fact, I was kind of looking forward to getting him out of the house so I could get some stuff done!"

Richard laughs. "She didn't see herself as a missions-trip person."

"No way," Grace confirms. "I assumed the women went along to do the cooking and the laundry. I've never been too great at so-called 'women stuff' and I really don't want people seeing me that way. So I just assumed I wouldn't fit in during a typical missions trip."

Richard interrupts at this point. "Once she found out she didn't have to cook, she was totally okay with coming along on a construction project," he tells us. "And now that she's been on four trips, you can't keep her at home!"

Grace found her first place of service as a bricklayer and mortar-mixer, helping build walls that became the foundation for Sunday-school classrooms for a church in southern Europe. Since then, she's learned other skills as well.

Near to Home

Serving others doesn't have to mean buying airline tickets and flying across an ocean. Helping others can happen in a variety of ways.

Tim and Jamie love to work with Habitat for Humanity.

"I did a Habitat project while I was in college," says Jamie.

"It was totally about helping a family get a new home. I spent my entire spring break up on the rafters of a house doing roofing work—which I'd never done in my life! After just one project with Habitat, I was hooked."

When Jamie married Tim, a divorced man with two young sons, she hoped that she and Tim might be able to work on a Habitat project together. They planned ahead and managed to schedule the same week of vacation with each of their employers. Tim's parents volunteered to watch the grandkids.

"We couldn't have done this without Tim's parents," Jamie says, beaming. "They've been absolutely wonderful for us, helping us have 'date nights' and giving us a break from parenting once in a while. When they spent a whole week with the boys, it was amazing. Tim and I were able to go down to Florida and build a house with Habitat without having to worry about the boys and how they were doing."

Did the experience bring the couple closer together?

"Are you kidding me?" Tim asks. "That was the best week of our marriage so far. I really saw a different side of Jamie that week."

Although they didn't always work side by side, spending a week at the same construction site meant they took their breaks together, ate their lunches together, and rode to and from work together in a Habitat van.

"We were sweating together big-time," remarks Jamie with a laugh. "In a weird way, somehow we got a lot closer to each other during that week. It was hot and muggy and we both got sunburned, but we didn't care! We were working for others, not for ourselves."

SOUP KITCHENS, FOOD PANTRIES for the homeless, prison ministries, and many other kinds of service projects are frequently organized by churches, synagogues, and parish ministry committees. If you're looking for a way to serve other people and to work together while you do it, you probably won't need to leave your own local community. The projects are ready and waiting: you just need to sign up!

Working together to serve others keeps your focus on the broader needs of the world around you. The vast majority of projects available, even construction projects, do not require you to have a specific job-related skill. If you can lift, carry, load, drive, and so on, there are plenty of opportunities to be useful.

In a smaller-scale project, perhaps sponsored by your own local church, it may be possible to serve together as an entire family. Some projects welcome the presence of children and have age-appropriate duties for everyone. When Faith Nazarene Church of Minneapolis, Minnesota, sent a construction team to Casal Novo, Portugal, four very young children were part of the team. Far from being a detriment to the project, the children— including a two-year-old girl with bright red hair—helped to break down the barriers between the American work crew and the host team from the local area. People passing by on the street would stop to admire or greet the children, and this conversation led to much interaction about the nature of the project, the identity of the church being built, and other things.

Serving others together side by side can strengthen the connection between a wife and husband, and between parents and children as well.

Take Time to Worship Together

We could easily have made worship the starting point for this chapter. It's the simplest activity to begin and continue, and it requires the least involvement and commitment of any of the topics we've discussed.

For exactly those reasons, we've saved worship until last. It's possible, for example, for a husband and wife to attend church together yet remain emotionally distant and spiritually separate during the entire service. From the platform, it's possible every week to look out across the sanctuary or auditorium and see couples who may be sitting side by side, yet are not "connecting" in any sense.

It may not have the bonding power of shared prayer, small-group interaction, or service projects, yet attending worship together is a valuable and meaningful step in helping a remarried couple establish its new identity.

The most difficult part may be deciding which church to attend! Often, remarried couples with children will select a church based on the kids' needs, especially if they are adolescents or teens. Churches with solid, biblically based, highly effective youth ministries are favored by remarried couples for the obvious reason that children and teens in a blended family are coping with stress on many levels. Helping teens deal with stress is just one function of an effective and life-changing youth ministry.

A Great Way to Bond

When Carol and Wayne remarried, they decided to attend Carol's church together. A primary factor in their decision was the fact that Carol's three kids, two of whom were teens, were well-established in their church youth group.

When the middle-school age group held a "father daughter" activity, Wayne was thrilled that Carol's daughter invited him to attend. "I had read about it in the church newsletter. But I didn't say anything, because I wasn't sure how Emily really felt about me in this new role as her stepfather," Wayne admits. "I thought she might skip the event altogether—or perhaps she might invite her dad, who lives nearby with his new wife and new family.

"Instead, Emily invited me. I couldn't believe how my heart 'jumped' when she sat down with us on a Saturday night after church and said, 'Wayne, will you go to Father–Daughter Night with me?'"

He gets emotional just talking about it.

Carol interjects her thoughts. "I didn't coach Emily about this at all. I had seen the same announcement in the newsletter also, and I wondered how she would feel. I couldn't decide whether to talk to her about it or just leave it alone. She didn't ask my advice or talk to me about it. She just sat down with us in the kitchen one Saturday night after church and asked Wayne to go with her."

It's Carol's turn to get emotional. "I think that was the start of our real bonding as a family," she says, dabbing at a tear in the corner of her eye.

Regardless of how a church is chosen, the key is to choose one. Honoring the idea of Sabbath, and honoring God by choosing to attend services of worship, is central to the spiritual foundation of a lasting remarriage.

Rest and Renewal Together

Kellie and Jackson are absolutely devoted to Saturday-night worship at their church.

"It's a second marriage for me," Jackson says, "and my first wife and I really didn't attend church very often. We were members of a large traditional church that she had been raised in, but somehow I never felt comfortable there. After we were married in that big, beautiful church building, we rarely went back.

"From the start, it was different with Kellie. She was totally about church and the things of God. She made it clear, after we began a relationship, that she would never get serious about anyone unless he was committed to God."

Kellie smiles. "I guess he believed me," she laughs. "After all, I wasn't kidding!"

She guessed that after a long absence from church attendance, her husband might be more comfortable attending a Saturday-night service. It was the start of what's proved to be a consistent pattern for the couple. At the large suburban church they attend, they can dress very casually on Saturday night. Feeling relaxed and at ease, instead of dressed-up and tense, was crucial to Jackson's involvement in worship.

"At first, I thought all the emotion was just phony," he

explains. "Seeing all that energy for the first time, with everyone smiling so constantly, I had to wonder if it was all for real. But two years later, I can't imagine trying to go back to a formal, more dressy kind of church service. It just wouldn't work! Kellie and I are planning to keep on attending Saturday night even if we start having children."

Whether Saturday night or Sunday morning, whether in a large church or small one, and regardless of the style, the key is to participate in worship together as a couple. Especially in the early days of a remarriage, be wary of making commitments to duties that take you apart, such as nursery work, Sunday-school-class teaching, and kitchen help. Instead, make it a point to be involved in worship together and to serve in other areas as a couple, working side by side rather than splitting up.

As it becomes a pattern and a habit, the Sabbath concept can function as God intended: as a day and time of rest and renewal, restoring our spiritual energy for the certain demands of the busy week ahead.

> **Forming a Spiritual Connection: The Four Key Activities**
>
> Here are four important ways you can nourish a meaningful spiritual connection as a remarried couple, so that your new marriage is focused on God:
>
> 1. Take time to pray together
> 2. Take time to learn together
> 3. Take time to serve together
> 4. Take time to worship together
>
> The Center for Marriage & Family Studies
> Del Mar, California

WHEN REMARRIED COUPLES CENTER their new relationship on honoring God, when they jointly establish Christ as the foundation of their home, positive things begin to happen. Relationships grow and thrive when serving God is a unifying priority for a remarried couple. Marriages are only as solid as their foundations; the best foundation is Jesus Christ.

Fred & Verna Beffa

A Long-Term Remarriage
Graced by God's Presence

VERNA WAS 18 YEARS OLD on her wedding day. Four years later she found herself busy raising two young children, a son and a daughter, while struggling to cope with a husband whose steady drinking was an ever-increasing problem.

When sober, her husband could be reasoned with and talked to. Drinking, he was mean-tempered and violent. Believing in the sanctity of marriage, and trying to make things work out for the best, Verna stayed committed to the relationship.

Her husband's drinking went from bad to worse, as did his behavior. Finally, fearing for her children and for her own safety, Verna reluctantly agreed to end the marriage. It was a sad and difficult time—a low point in her life.

She wasn't certain she could love again. She wasn't eager to risk another relationship after the suffering and loss of her first marriage.

Then, by the grace of God, her life took an unexpected turn.

In May 1947, not long after the end of World War II, Verna walked the aisle a second time, having accepted a marriage proposal from Fred Beffa, three years her senior, who had not previously been married.

Six years into her second marriage, Verna had given birth two more times; another son and another daughter. This second set of children was almost a whole generation apart from her older children, who were already in their late teens.

Everything about the new relationship was different and

better. Verna found herself happier and more fulfilled than ever before.

The couple raised the daughter from Verna's first marriage, in addition to raising the son and daughter of their own union. In the 1960s, the family moved from Tennessee to Wisconsin, putting down roots and forming a long-term, stable household and family circle.

By the 1970s, as the last of their children graduated from high school and left for college, Fred and Verna were active in their church and their community, widely known and widely respected for the strength of their marriage relationship. The depth of their commitment was readily apparent in the way they looked at each other, spoke to each other, and treated each other. Married now for 25 years, they were empty-nesters, happy, and in love.

In May 1997, we were privileged to be invited to Rice Lake, Wisconsin, for a joyous occasion—the golden wedding anniversary of a spry and still youthful couple—Fred and Verna Beffa.

By the late 1990s, 50-year anniversaries were rare enough in original marriages, and a 50-year anniversary for a remarriage was even more distinctive and worthy of special recognition and honor.

With their children and grandchildren gathered around them, Fred and Verna celebrated the goodness of God and the warmth of friends and family. Cake and candles were set out as the community gathered for a celebration.

With twinkles in their eyes, this obviously romantic duo enjoyed the moment, giving God the credit for their long and positive union. Laughter and gratitude punctuated a time of remembering and sharing.

Six years later, just a few days before his ninety-third birthday, Fred died. By then, almost 56 years had passed since he and Verna had said, "I do." They were still a shining example of married love and godly commitment.

AMONG OUR FRIENDS, FAMILIES, AND CLIENTS, Fred and Verna are the current "record holders" for the longest-lasting remarriage. Yet their union was not merely lengthy—it was deep and positive, exemplifying all that is good about serving God, being married, and raising a family.

How long have you been remarried? Whether it's been ten days or ten years, be encouraged by the positive, real-life experience of Fred and Verna Beffa.

CHAPTER THREE

Principle Number Two

Regard Your Remarriage as Permanent and Irreversible

❁

He who desires to see the living God
face-to-face should not seek him
in the empty firmament of his mind,
but in human love.

FYODOR DOSTOEVSKY

WHEN A REMARRIAGE IS PERMANENT, you can't just "give up" on it.

Walking through central Philadelphia a few years ago, we encountered homeless people living in cardboard boxes: big-screen-TV boxes, refrigerator boxes, all sorts of large boxes. As the icy winter winds sliced through downtown, people slept on the sidewalks, surrounded only by their flimsy cardboard shacks.

Chances are if you're reading this book, you've got a much better bed to sleep in tonight and a much finer roof over your head. But what if your home *was* a large cardboard box? And more to the point, what if you knew for certain this very same cardboard box was the only home you would ever have as long as you lived?

With no hope of moving to an urban loft or a trendy condo, how would you react? Human nature suggests one thing: You'd do everything in your power to make that cardboard box as cozy, comfortable, warm, dry, and safe as you possibly could.

You would do everything imaginable. You'd get carpet scraps or an old rug to line the floor. You'd find some fabric and insulate the walls. To make it yours, you would decorate with paint, chalk, or any available medium. One way or another, you'd make that box into a place called "home."

You'd give it your very best since after all, you'd be stuck in that box for the rest of your life. You'd upgrade, redecorate, and refurbish it every chance you got—you'd want it to be as good as it could possibly be.

That's what you do when you're "stuck" with something forever.

Now, think beyond the box!

This book begins where you're already living—and explores how to move forward from that point. Whether this is your second marriage or your fifth, this book is here to help you make your current marriage your "last" one—the one that lasts. As this happens, new patterns that honor God will be established, patterns that point effectively to His redemption and His grace.

This book is written to help you succeed and "go the distance" in your relationship—to help you and your current spouse grow together in mature, lasting, and committed love.*

When you regard your remarriage as permanent and irreversible, several important changes begin to take root in your relationship. Each of these helps to build a strong positive value into your life, replacing negative experiences and ideas that may have carried over from your past patterns.

---

* If you have not remarried, use this book to prayerfully consider the challenges you'll be facing in a remarriage environment. There are a lot of compelling reasons to remain single as you raise your children. Though difficult, being a single parent may be God's best plan for you and your family.

You're More Likely to Work
Through the Tough Times

When you regard a remarriage as temporary, as something that might or might not succeed, you're creating an "escape clause" that can take the place of hard work. In the back of your mind, you're allowing for the possibility that, if this person isn't right for you, the next one might be.

That kind of thinking dooms a remarriage right from the start. It leads to shallow relationships, only partially pursued, that never achieve their highest potential or their deepest value. At some level, whether you know it or not, you are holding back from the kind of deep commitment that defines a lasting and fruitful partnership. Part of you continues thinking about another "new start" if needed.

In contrast, when you regard a remarriage as permanent, you begin to realize if you want to be happy, if you want to be involved in a successful relationship, you'd better get to work: This is the only marriage you'll ever have! And that attitude, all by itself, has the power to work wonders in your union.

> **How It Helps Your Relationship to Consider It Permanent and Irreversible**
>
> Regarding your remarriage as permanent...
>
> 1. makes you more likely to work through the tough times and solve problems.
> 2. helps you create a sense of success in your relationship and identity.
> 3. establishes a powerful example for your children and family.
>
> The Center for Marriage & Family Studies
> Del Mar, California

A Powerful Behavioral Tool

When we work with remarried couples in a secular setting, we often start with this concept instead of the spiritual topics from the previous chapter. This is not an effort to hide our religious orientation—we're very open about our beliefs. Instead, we begin with this point because, apart from God and a life of faith, this is the strongest behavioral tool we know of to build and strengthen a remarriage.

Judy and Carl are living proof. Married before either one of them professed any religious inclinations, both had been married previously. Both, as they discovered while getting acquainted, felt like they were failures as a consequence of being divorced. Both were single parents, raising younger children with very little help from the ex-spouse.

"I wasn't willing to go through that again," Carl explains, speaking of the end of his marriage. "I was either going to stay single or else remarry for life—as far as I was concerned, there was no other option."

Judy felt the same way. "A lot of my friends advised me to stay single. And I really understood what they meant. The last thing on earth I wanted was to have another marriage start off well, seem to be promising, then crash and burn. I was afraid to remarry because I was afraid to watch another marriage fail.

"Carl and I talked about that for a long time. Neither one of us was afraid of being single, but both of us hated the thought of another divorce. The only reason we didn't just move in together was that the older children were getting toward their teen years and we didn't want to set that kind of example for them."

With the aid of a family therapist, Carl and Judy talked openly and deeply about their expectations for a remarriage. They both decided up front that if they chose to remarry, it would be for a lifetime—regardless of consequences. That decision became a powerful force in the emerging remarriage, setting them up for success and satisfaction in their relationship. Without attaching any kind of religious commitment to the event, the couple pledged themselves to each other for life as their children watched and listened.

"We were serious anyway," Carl explains. "But once we had made those vows in front of the children, who were old enough to understand what they were hearing, there was no way we were *ever* going to end our remarriage!'"

Carl and Judy approached their relationship as the last one they would ever experience. They invested in it as their "home" for life—making it as good as it could possibly be.

Did that make Carl and Judy's relationship trouble-free? Far from it. Just two years into the remarriage, both were frustrated, worn out, and tired of trying to make the relationship "click."

"No matter what we tried, we just weren't relating very well," Judy says about that difficult point. "I felt like Carl wasn't attached enough to my children, like he didn't really care deeply about them.

"He felt I wasn't doing my share of keeping house and making our family schedule work for everyone. He felt he was carrying the load all by himself. We started to fight over small things—not really yelling at each other—but complaining, criticizing, and arguing all the time."

Carl is nodding his head as his wife speaks.

"Frankly, I thought I'd made another mistake," he admits. "Even though I'd been really careful before committing to marriage, perhaps I hadn't been careful enough. I was tired of trying all the time. I felt nothing was working."

What kept the couple together?

"Just one thing," Judy explains with a wry smile. "We had both decided this relationship was permanent. Whether it worked well or not, it was going to endure and last forever. Basically, we had agreed beforehand that, one way or another, we were both stuck with each other."

"If we hadn't done that, I probably would have walked," Carl confesses. "Not to blame anyone other than myself, but things just weren't working out." He goes on to tell the story of how he and Judy later converted to Christianity through the influence of some close friends and that, these days, God is really helping their remarriage thrive and succeed.

"But," Judy insists, "with or without God, and whether our remarriage was going well or going badly, we'd still be together either way. We looked each other in the eyes, spoke the words out loud in front of our children and our friends, and made a decision that this marriage—for better or for worse—was for always."

A Place for Relationship Investment

When a husband and wife insist their remarriage is permanent and irreversible, they have taken an important step toward longevity and fruitfulness. Knowing that each partner is committed, come what may, helps each person feel safer and more secure.

For those who have experienced the dissolution of a prior marriage, it is vitally important to reconnect with the "'til death do us part" dimension of the commitment. When both members of a remarriage understand there is no escape clause—no way out, no option other than staying together—a powerful and positive signal is received in the subconscious mind of each partner. This signal is a strong agent of behavioral change.

When your remarried spouse becomes your "partner for life" in every sense of the phrase, your marriage becomes a place where energy is invested to make the relationship the best it can possibly be. It can exhibit just as much strength, endurance, and longevity as the best of "original" marriages—just as much passion, security, and richness in the minds and hearts of both partners.

You'll Build a Sense of Success into Your Relationship

A sense of success comes from a "paradigm shift" from failure and frustration to growth and generosity. As we work with women who have experienced the end of a marriage, one of the most common themes that emerges is a profound sense of personal failure. Remarkably, even when a woman ascribes most of the blame to her ex-husband, she still manages to internalize a strong sense of shame and regret over her own shortcomings. This can be true even in cases where the wife has been abandoned by a straying husband or deserted by an irresponsible one.

Men seem far less likely to blame themselves for the end of a relationship and are also much less likely to develop a self-image that centers in personal failure. A man can divorce several times in a row without considering himself at fault. Yet within such a man's unexplored conscience and personal identity, there may be significant traces of guilt, self-doubt, and remorse.

As a remarriage survives its "growing pains" and begins to thrive, a sense of success can begin to replace the previous feelings of failure and inadequacy. In both partners, but particularly in the woman, a greater sense of self-worth and self-esteem begins to develop. The roots of this change vary, but the common theme is a newfound sense of personal competency.

FOR PAIGE, IT WAS ALL ABOUT THE KIDS. "My first husband and I did not have children," she explains. "It was one of the many ways our relationship just didn't work out. When I married Gary, he had three kids from his previous marriage. Scary? I had never even been a mother before, and now I felt like I was competing with the birth mother of three children I didn't even know."

Gary constantly assured her otherwise. "The kids already have a mother. Just be yourself, get to know them at your own pace, and don't try to be superwoman!"

It was the best advice Paige ever received.

"It took about a thousand times of Gary saying that before I really listened," she confides. "I kept feeling I needed to be the world's most perfect mother for these kids, or else they wouldn't like me. That didn't work, by the way, but Gary kept telling me to forget about it.

"They'd come back from a visit with their mom and they'd be talking about all the fun things they'd done together, and I felt so jealous! That would cause me to try even harder to win them over. But every time I tried, it just didn't work. I was so worn out, so frustrated, so tired of failing to be the perfect mother I desperately wanted to be.

"One night, after the kids were all in bed, Gary sat down with me and very gently told me he had married a wife, not a mother. He told me to let go of all my efforts to 'mother' the kids. He asked me to focus on being his wife and let the kids figure things out for themselves."

Why did she listen this time, and not before?

"I guess I was tired of failing all the time," she says. "Although Gary had been saying the same thing constantly since we got married, this time I listened and understood what he meant."

In the days that followed, Paige relaxed and tried to let go of her sense of "duty" and "performance" about being a mother to three children. Instead, she devoted herself to being a happy, supportive companion to her husband.

"Here's the weird thing," Paige tells us with a smile. "As soon as I quit trying to be a wonderful mother, the kids started opening up to me. I still don't understand it, but that's exactly how it happened! They would still come home and talk about fun things they had done at their mom's, but I just listened and didn't let it bother me. It wasn't about me anymore. I wasn't competing with anyone, certainly not with their birth mother."

Gary comments, "I think when you relax about things, instead of pushing so hard, it's easier for everybody to find their place, and work things out."

How long does that process take?

For this couple, it was about three years after their remarriage. Paige spent more than a year striving—and failing—to be supermom. It took a year or so more after that before the new family began to function as a unit.

When things finally started to gel, Paige didn't see it coming. "I was making school lunches one day, in the kitchen, very early, and our youngest son came downstairs all sleepy," she remembers, dabbing at a tear. "He climbed up on a bar stool by where I was standing, gave me a big hug, and said 'Mom, can I help you?' "

She pauses to regain her composure. "It was the first time any of them called me 'Mom,' and I can't tell you how wonderful that felt! I hugged him and started crying. He didn't know why, and he even asked me if I was okay. I told him I was very happy…that sometimes moms cry when they're happy. I don't know if he understood that or not, but we shared a long hug and then we finished making three lunches together.

"We were 'mother and son' that morning in the kitchen, and suddenly I began to feel like the successful mom I had always wanted to be. And ironically, it started once I quit trying!"

"My kids love her," Gary says proudly. "And by the way, gradually all three of them started calling her 'Mom'—which we never asked them to do."

How does Paige feel today, as the mother of two teens and a youngest son who's now in his "tween" years?

"I've got a long way to go," she laughs. "But honestly, I finally feel almost successful at this wife and mother thing. My husband didn't give up on me, and I'm glad he just patiently kept giving me good advice. For the first time in my adult life, I might actually have my act together in some ways—"

"Don't let her fool you," Gary interrupts. "She's doing great!"

Optimism Takes Over

When a remarriage begins to establish itself as a permanent entity, both partners begin to exude a sense of confidence and energy that is contagious and highly positive. A sense of success begins to pervade the self-image and self-awareness of both partners, replacing the previous paradigm of failure and shame.

This optimism is powerful, helping each spouse replace old fears with new hopes. As the old saying goes, "Nothing succeeds like success." And when a relationship establishes itself as permanent, both partners benefit from the sense of being successful.

FOR RICK, IT FELT LIKE COMING HOME. "I had been married three times. I'd had children with two of my ex-wives. I was a runaway husband and an absentee dad, never really there for my children as they grew up," he laments. "I felt terrible unless I was drinking, so I drank all the time. When my third marriage ended, I decided I'd never marry again. I threw a few things in my Dodge pickup truck, drove west, and basically just ran away from reality.

"I met Carla in a bar, but she was working there—not drinking. She was waitressing to make extra money. Even though I was drunk all the time, I wasn't too drunk to notice her and be attracted to her."

Carla, single and nearing 30, had never been married before. The idea of marrying a three-time loser and full-time alcoholic was out of the question.

"He didn't actually propose marriage to me," she laughs. "His proposal was to live together, not to get married. But to me, it was all the same either way. Or in other words—no way!"

Intrigued by the rejection, Rick tried even harder to win Carla's affection. He kept coming back to the bar, not just to drink but also to be around her. She kept declining his offers of "romance," but he wouldn't take no for an answer.

Eventually, Rick began asking what it would take to win her heart.

Over a period of months, "She just laid it out there," Rick grins. "It wasn't good enough to be sober, I also had to be employed, making decent money, and behaving like an adult."

It's Carla's turn to laugh. "I wasn't trying to be hard to get—I wanted to be impossible."

Rick fooled them both. Less than ten months after meeting Carla at the bar, Rick was several months sober and newly employed. He signed a lease on a new townhouse in a family-oriented neighborhood with parks, ball fields, and a community pool.

At that point, Carla consented to go out with him.

"I had found God through an AA class," he recalls, "and I was truly trying to live for Him—in my own way. But I still wanted Carla to move in with me, and she wouldn't do it. She wouldn't even have sex with me!"

Carla confirms this. "I wasn't really religious at that point. I wasn't trying to be a perfect person; I just wanted to be sure Rick had truly changed."

By the grace of God, change happens. Two years after meeting Carla for the first time, Rick said "I do" in front of a minister and a small group of friends from his newfound church. For the first time in his life, the words carried serious meaning for him.

"I know I've made a lot of mistakes in my life," he admits. "And I wish I could make up for all of that, but I can't. The amazing thing is, I feel like I'm married for the very first time. I feel like I'm a husband for the first time, and every time I walk in the door, I get this feeling of 'coming home.'"

Instead of running away, Rick finds himself running home. Together, he and Carla have created an atmosphere of success in his life and in their married life.

You'll Set a Powerful New Example for Your Children

In your remarriage, you have the opportunity to show your children that it's never too late for "forever."

Margaret and her first husband fought constantly. At first

verbal, the arguments later became physical. There was no "abuse" of one partner by the other; instead, their fights were equal parts give-and-take, with each one dishing it out, and each one taking it.

"When our baby was born, I really thought we'd change," Margaret recalls. "I didn't want us to be fighting all the time in front of our baby, but we were. We didn't know how to deal with each other, except to fight."

The marriage lasted through five stormy years and produced two children. By the time it ended, both partners were ready to separate. The divorce proceeding was friendlier and more positive than the marriage had ever been. Margaret's husband relocated out of state. He seldom returned to see his family, but when he did, the couple fell into old patterns, arguing and fighting.

Margaret sighs. "I always wanted to protect my kids. But the truth is, all they ever saw was Mom and Dad fighting, then Dad leaving. All they knew about marriage was that people get mad and argue all the time—and then they leave."

She and her ex-husband had set a powerful example for their two children, but not the kind she had hoped to provide.

Margaret remarried almost immediately, wedding an older man whose children were grown and living on their own. David, a widower, had experienced a lengthy and healthy marriage relationship.

The two partners brought two very different marriage patterns into their new relationship. David and his first wife had resolved issues peacefully, discussed things openly, and raised their children in a positive, caring environment.

Margaret's children had grown up listening to arguing and fighting—watching their parents push, shove, hit, scratch, and sometimes bite each other. Which pattern would establish itself in the new relationship?

"I can't take any credit for the way my life is now. David gets all the credit, in my book," Margaret insists. "He's been such a loving father to my two children and such a great husband to me."

New Patterns Start to Take Hold

When a remarriage relationship is established in an atmosphere of commitment and permanence, children slowly begin to trust the stability of the new family unit. The key things to note here are *trust* and *slowly.*

"I'm sure my kids didn't know what to expect," admits Margaret. "All they'd ever seen had been noise and messiness, right from the start. I suppose they thought David was going to be my new boxing partner!"

Instead, the newlyweds followed a pattern that more consistently mirrored that of David's prior marriage. Free and open discussion preceded any major decisions. Arguing and fighting became a thing of the past.

"I noticed one change in my kids right away," Margaret says. "Their volume level decreased almost immediately. I hadn't realized how noisy they were—probably because I couldn't hear them over the sound of my own fighting with my ex-husband. Even their talking voices dropped down a few notches. Also, they fought with each other a lot less."

Gradually but surely, the new patterns began to take hold.

Today, nearly ten years after their remarriage, Margaret and David are setting a powerful example for their children—this time, exactly the kind of example Margaret always hoped to set: Mom and Dad love each other, relate well to each other, and are committed to each other for life.

"I worried it was already too late for my kids, too late to start setting any new examples," she relates. "But what I've seen is just the opposite: They've grown up watching David and me get along really well."

David declines credit for how well the children are doing. "I love both of them very much," he says of the kids, "but one thing I decided from the start was that Margaret would do the parenting. That gave us one less thing to possibly fight about—discipline of the kids. I supported any decision Margaret made whether I agreed with it or not. The kids saw us as a united front—their mom made the decisions, and I supported her."

Margaret smiles at that. "I think I wanted him to do more parenting, at first," she reveals. "I was tired of being the grown-up, tired of coping on my own after my husband left us. Later, I saw the wisdom of David's choice. Instead of trying to be the new boss and the new daddy, he came into the relationship as my husband."

David chuckles. "The kids kept testing me. I stayed slow and steady, trying to be really patient with them, and I kept backing up every decision Margaret made."

Slowly and steadily, the new pattern took hold. The children saw that Mom and her husband didn't fight, didn't argue, didn't yell, didn't push each other. An attitude of kindness and fairness prevailed in household discussions.

And Margaret and David constantly reinforced the basic underlying certainty: They had married for life—and they planned to stay together forever.

It's Not Too Late for Your Kids

Heather believed it was too late. "My kids had seen me walk out of two marriages. And in between they'd seen several live-in boyfriends come and go," Heather confesses. "In terms of setting an example for them, I'd been the worst mom in the world."

A third marriage caught her by surprise. A co-worker had become a friend, gradually spending more and more time with her and her children. Not sensing anything romantic, Heather relaxed and enjoyed the friendship, never expecting anything further to develop.

Jared's proposal was a complete surprise. Even more surprising, Jared had talked with Heather's kids in advance. They had been excited about the idea and had managed to keep the "big secret" from their mother for three whole days.

When Jared got down on his knees in the middle of their

favorite pizza parlor, Heather was the last to find out. She found herself completely speechless.

Heather laughs in remembering. "I think at first I was just in total shock, then I started crying. I don't know what Jared was thinking or the kids were thinking, but I couldn't even think! I didn't believe what was happening to me!"

Her kids gave her some help. "Tell him yes, Mom!" nine-year-old Joshua insisted loudly.

Heather followed her son's advice, accepting Jared's proposal and his slipping a simple, inexpensive engagement ring onto her finger.

"Jared knew I'd had expensive jewelry—and lousy relationships—with both of my two husbands," she says, smiling. "I had joked with him, just in friendship, that next time I wanted cheap jewelry and a really great relationship!"

She got both. Now married for almost eight years, Heather talks about the new, life-changing example she and Jared are setting for the children.

"I thought it was too late for them," she sighs. "But looking back, it almost seems like Jared and I have been together for the kids' whole lives. We've been blessed that they seem well-adjusted and happy. Also, I think it helped a lot that they knew Jared before we got married and already liked him.

"Most of all," she adds reflectively, "Jared and I have worked to convince them we're together forever. We're not going to split up; he's not leaving us. The way we say it is, 'No matter what happens, we're a family forever!' We've got the kids saying that to *us* now, any time they think Jared and I are having an argument or starting to fight a little bit. It's cute—sometimes in an annoying way—but it helps us remember we're in this for good."

Just like Margaret and David, Heather and Jared have learned that treating your remarriage as permanent puts a powerful, positive example in front of your children. Over time, it begins to replace their previous ideas about marriage with more hopeful views.

Ronald & Nancy Reagan

An Enduring Love Survives
50 Years of Challenges

HE WAS MARRIED FOR NEARLY A DECADE; they shared a common interest and career in filmmaking. Their union produced a daughter by birth and a son by adoption, and the couple also lost a daughter.

She filed for the divorce—neither of them ever publicly commented on its causes or its reasons. Instead, they remained amicable and cared capably for their two children. Both continued to work in their chosen professions. Both continued to move in the same circle of friends, acquaintances, and co-workers.

Three years after the divorce he found the courage to marry again. He had met Nancy on a blind date arranged by a mutual friend. After two years of steady dating, he proposed to her at Chasen's restaurant. She accepted, opening the first chapter of a lifelong romance that even the pair's critics came to greatly admire.

Thus was born one of the most committed and loving unions of our time. And for the record, this enduring romance bloomed within a second marriage.

For Ron, this second marriage would become his last one, spanning more than five decades, ending only at his death. He would love and cherish his wife. Along the way, the remarried couple would have two children of their own, a son and a daughter, while enjoying a remarkable career in public life.

For Nancy, this marriage would in some ways reflect the experience of her mother. She had married a man, Dr. Loyal

Davis, who had previously been divorced. Nancy had witnessed, in person, a second marriage that became a strong and lasting union.

The Reagans' devotion to each other would become legendary, a fact noted by biographers, family members, close friends, and staff members. Ron would talk of becoming lonely "when she left the room." When traveling on business, he'd send love notes, flowers, gifts, and warm personal letters.

They began with a simple wedding, small and private. The only witnesses were a close friend, actor William Holden, and his wife, Ardis.

Their marriage, however, would become a major part of their public persona and image, actively examined and written about by the press. It would be witnessed by television viewers, by the residents of California, and later by the citizens of the United States and the world.

The marriage would grow and thrive.

Ronnie and Nancy. Together.

It's impossible to picture one without the other. Riding on horseback through the trails of their mountain ranch. Arm in arm at a state dinner or some other government event. He'd be speaking, perhaps, and the camera would pan back to reveal Nancy, listening, her eyes rapt with attention, her face shining with obvious (and very real) admiration for her husband.

He would spend eight years hosting a weekly television program. He'd serve two terms as governor of the most populous state of the United States. Eventually he would also serve two terms as president of the U.S., surviving an assassination attempt early in his service to the nation.

Then, as always, Nancy would be at his side. They would share a devotion to each other that never wavered, never waned, never expired. Time would only deepen the bond between them, only reinforce the commitment that held them so closely together.

LIFE WAS DIFFICULT AT TIMES. He battled and survived colon cancer. She fought and triumphed over breast cancer. Whatever they faced, whatever life dealt them, they met it together with bravery and with firm resolve.

Failing to gain a nomination in his first run for the presidency, Ron, with Nancy, returned four years later to win one of the largest electoral victories of modern times. Simply put, they wouldn't quit, wouldn't give up, wouldn't abandon the dream.

It was that way in their marriage also; they were committed forever.

For 52 years, a nation and the world watched as this long-term remarried couple defined commitment and romance, showering each other with respect, affection, and open admiration. Both political supporters and opponents acknowledged that the romance was real, the commitment genuine, the love true.

In the end, Nancy would care for her husband tirelessly, rarely leaving his side, tending their love faithfully despite the challenge of his Alzheimer's disease. Ron would slip away quietly, leaving his legacy in films and public service.

His legacy would include, also, a shining example of commitment and love within a second marriage.

CHAPTER FOUR

Principle Number Three

Forgive Everyone,
Including Yourself

❋

*That there is true greatness in making concessions,
that forgiveness is a real victory, and that
to renounce one's own will is a true joy—these are
ideas which have almost disappeared today.*

PAUL TOURNIER

OVER THE ROAR OF A TYPICAL family Saturday morning, Reggie dropped his bomb.

"I just need my space for a while," he began, not waiting for a quiet moment or a strategic pause. "It's only for a while, but I need to do this for me."

Denise's hands trembled; she set a juice pitcher down on the counter and stared intently at her husband. Married for five years, she and Reggie shared three children and a marriage that seemed better than many of those around them. They quarreled and fought sometimes, but things never became violent.

Reggie wants his space? What's this about?

"I just need to do this for me," he said again. Then, without waiting for comments or questions, he walked out the door. It would be a week before Denise saw him or heard from him again: a week of wondering and waiting, fielding constant inquiries from the children and from everyone else.

Several months after that fateful Saturday morning, Denise learned the shocking truth. Her husband had been involved with another woman almost from the beginning of their marriage. Five years after marrying her, Reggie had three children within his marriage and two children outside of it, with the other partner. By announcing he "wanted his space," he was in fact changing homes and moving in with his other family unit. He was choosing the other woman, the other children, the other apartment.

Denise, an active churchgoer and devoutly religious person, reacted with stunned disbelief. Things like this only happened on soap operas, not in reality! She was in shock, unable to accept Reggie's abandonment as the truth. How could she have lived with a man for five years and never known about his other life?

She struggled to understand what was happening. Nothing made sense. As the shock gradually wore off, anger took its place. Denise found herself filled with massive amounts of rage. While driving along the freeway, she'd catch herself swearing under her breath—and she didn't swear! When people asked about her husband, she would explode with angry comments and bitter complaints.

"I had dreams about killing him," she admits today. "I couldn't have actually done it, of course, but I had dreams about it. I'd wake up feeling guilty, but relieved at the same time. I couldn't believe what Reggie had done to us!"

After the initial denial wore off, a long season of rage began. The couple divorced. It would be eight years before Denise would even consider being in a marriage relationship, eight years during which she raised her three children as a single mother, struggling with finances constantly.

Anger happens. For Denise, it happened daily for eight years.

Anger—Valid but Not Permanent

In many situations, anger is a correct and valid response. How should Denise be expected to feel, given Reggie's behavior?

Her feelings of rage, betrayal, disappointment, and bitterness were completely authentic and normal.

In its initial stages, anger serves physiological purposes that are positive. It unleashes a flow of energy that helps us make decisions, take action, and move forward. Without the energy anger provides, many of us would remain "frozen" in our denial and avoidance, unable to make needed choices and changes.

Yet anger, while natural and valid, is not intended to be a permanent state. Indeed, holding onto anger over a period of time poisons our health physically as well as emotionally, weakening our body's natural immune system and leaving us vulnerable to illness and disease.

"Do not let your anger lead you into sin," Paul counsels in his letter to the church at Ephesus. "Do not stay angry all day" (Ephesians 4:26). A few verses later, he pens this postscript: "Get rid of all bitterness...and anger" (verse 31).

Anger becomes problematic when we cling to it, holding on instead of letting go. Unreleased anger pollutes our inner environment and prevents us from growing emotionally. Although it is likely to damage our relationship with others, its primary result is to damage *us*, both emotionally and physically.

Forgiving Others

The antidote to anger is forgiveness: the process of releasing our anger and frustration, thus restoring the inner health of our soul and spirit. Although difficult, forgiveness is critically important even when you have been greatly wronged.

Forgiveness is a conscious decision to let go of anger and move forward, regardless of the unfairness and injustice of the situation. It is the act of taking control of your own emotions, making your own decisions about values and choices and personal identity. It is the beginning of healing.

Denise felt used and betrayed. Her husband had entered a marriage contract with her yet had made no effort to treat the marriage as sacred or exclusive. She felt like the entire marriage had been a complete lie on his part. So she was angry. Yet one way or another, what she needed to do—for herself—was to find a way to forgive Reggie, leave the past behind, and move into the future.

It would be simpler, although still challenging, if the other party always asked (or begged!) for our forgiveness. In reality, this is seldom the case. Yet forgiveness is such essential work, for our own sakes, that it must not wait for tears and apologies from the one who has hurt or offended us. Besides, those tears and apologies may never occur.

In Denise's case, Reggie persisted in trying to have it both ways: He would drop by unannounced, trying to visit his children and hoping to bed his ex-wife. Every time he would visit, still claiming to love her but living with the other woman, Denise's anger would flare up all over again.

Gradually, she realized she needed to forgive Reggie for *her* sake, not for his. She realized her own emotions, including the tone and attitude with which she was raising her children, needed the healing power of forgiveness. So, although her ex-husband had not asked for it and in fact would not do so, she made a conscious decision to forgive him, turning her attention away from issues of the past and thinking about life in terms of the present and the future.

Paul recommends this kind of thinking to the Philippians: "The one thing I do, however, is to forget what is behind me and do my best to reach what is ahead" (Philippians 3:13). He is not denying the failures and difficulties of the past; rather, he is making a conscious choice to change his focus. Instead of thinking about what has gone wrong or has been painful, Paul is focusing in a forward direction.

In Denise's case, the change was radical and immediate.

"Once I decided to forgive him, it was like my whole body relaxed," she remembers. "I had been tensed up and angry for longer than I could remember." With the help of a sympathetic pastor and a few close friends, she affirmed her forgiveness in a circle of prayer, support, and accountability.

Reggie didn't even know he was forgiven; he hadn't asked to be.

"I didn't give him the privileges of a husband," Denise says, "since after all, he had chosen to leave all that! But I definitely changed my attitude toward him, something that happened inside my heart. I realized that, even if he never changed or grew up, I could forgive him and get on with my life."

GRANT'S SITUATION WAS even more complicated.

His wife left him—for another woman.

After 12 years of seemingly happy marriage, he was thoroughly adjusted to the routines of his workday and family life. He loved his children, cherished his wife, and in many ways was living his dream. The children were doing well at school and he was advancing in his career. Life was good.

He knew his wife, Marie, had been depressed; he knew also she was attending a women's therapy group to express her feelings. It didn't occur to him at any time that she might find herself drawn to another woman. He never imagined she might abandon him and the children, move out of their home, and embrace a completely new orientation and lifestyle.

He was confused and in shock. As these emotions gradually wore off, Grant found himself angrier than he'd ever been in his whole life. He started seeing a counselor, mostly so he'd have a safe place to yell, scream, complain, and release the anger that kept welling up inside of him.

"It wasn't so much that I was angry with my wife," he relates. "Somehow I saw her as a victim in this whole situation. I was angry with the woman who I believed had led my wife away from her family. For a long time after Marie left us, I couldn't be in the same room as her new partner. I found myself indulging in violent daydreams, imagining myself attacking or crushing this other woman. Every time I thought about her—which was often—my thoughts were dark."

Grant's counselor mostly listened at first, offering little by way of advice. Gradually, the counselor began to suggest that, for his own sake, Grant needed to forgive his wife, forgive her new partner, and begin to move forward. By this time, divorce proceedings were well in motion.

As Grant recounts, "I didn't want to hear it. I felt like the counselor was trying to make this *my* problem—even though I was the responsible one, I was in the right, I was the one who had stayed true to my spouse and my family."

The counselor focused on the needs of the children and on how Grant was to care for them. This was the turning point in the therapy.

"I didn't want to forgive anybody," Grant admits. "It was too early for that, in my view—not that I would ever have forgiven them, probably. But the counselor just wouldn't quit. He kept insisting I needed to forgive my wife, forgive her partner, let go of my rage, and start being a relaxed, cheerful parent for my kids. After all, the kids had struggles of their own to deal with!"

As the therapy continued, he found the emotional strength he needed to forgive his wife and the other woman. "That didn't make it any easier to be around my wife's new partner," Grant says. "I kept finding that difficult: in fact, I still do. But there was a real difference in my thought life, my emotional life, and really, in my whole way of looking at things. I quit thinking about the unfairness of it all and began to think instead about my kids—and about what *they* needed."

Preparation to Trust

Although both Grant and Denise had every reason to be suspicious of marriage and to avoid trying again, both eventually remarried: Denise after eight years and Grant after nearly three. Both affirm that forgiveness was an essential step in being ready for another relationship.

"If I hadn't forgiven Reggie, I could never have trusted anyone else," Denise says. "And I needed every one of those eight years to be ready."

Grant's perspective is similar. "No one would have found me attractive in my angry years. Emotionally, I was just one big quivering mass of anger, frustration, and hate. Letting go of all that helped me become the kind of person that someone else might find attractive, might want to be with."

Forgiveness was essential work both Grant and Denise needed to do, even if they'd chosen to remain single.

Forgiving Each Other in the New Relationship

Forgiveness is not just about former relationships. A remarried person constantly needs to be forgiving and accepting with his or her new partner.

Forgiveness is an essential social and relational skill for everyone, but especially so for remarried persons. Unpacking in a new home, each partner has brought more than the usual baggage across the threshold. Difficult patterns and troublesome relationships may have characterized the past marriage: How will the new couple relate and adjust?

Remarried persons need adaptability and an inclination to forgive others as key ingredients of the new relationship. They need a longer and more flexible adjustment period in setting up a new household and in forming a new family unit. They need to receive and grant forgiveness.

Issues from the past may erupt almost daily as a remarriage begins. A spouse who has been abandoned by her partner may cling too tightly to a new mate; she may be suspicious of him in irrational and unreasonable ways. As she learns to accept and trust him, she'll need to be forgiven for her lack of trust and her suspicion. Remarried persons are especially susceptible to issues of insecurity, fear, lack of trust, irrational worry, and other negative traits.

Forgiveness matters. As we travel to speak to remarried persons across the country, we are increasingly hopeful and optimistic about the strength of the remarriages we see. One reason is exactly the topic we've been discussing: people tend to be, on balance, a lot more forgiving of their partners the second time around.

Original marriages tend to begin with a high emotional component, with factors like physical attractiveness and romantic feelings playing a large role in the formation of the relationship. Many first marriages fall apart as the couples discover, after marriage, that they have major differences in values, beliefs, behaviors, and perspectives.

Remarriages tend to be more rationally based. They still have a strong romantic component, but the core attraction tends to be rooted in features deeper than outward appearance or emotional rushes. They are often based on a better understanding of compatible personality types, similarity of political or religious views, and life experiences that are similar—or they've begun as a close friendship. Such relationships have a head start from the beginning.

While some people remarry "on the rebound," many divorced persons are slow to form a new union. They take their time, being careful in choosing a compatible partner. Previously married people are more likely to consult others before entering a new union; original marriages, by contrast, are often a headlong rush to the altar. The advice of the partners' friends and family, and the opinions of their children, if any, tend to be important factors in a decision to remarry.

A Key Strategy

Ellen and Steve typify this slower, more careful approach to remarriage. Each had been married once before; each prior marriage had had a difficult ending. By common consent, they allowed a growing friendship to remain just that—a friendship—for a lengthy period of time. Then gradually, and with the help of a trained counselor, they began exploring the possibility of marriage.

Counseling helped them discover patterns of behavior that might need the power of forgiveness. For example, Steve tended to be impulsive and emotional in his purchasing decisions, even when large sums of money were involved. Ellen, who had been mired heavily in debt as a single parent, was cautious and highly conservative with her money.

"I needed those lessons on forgiveness!" Ellen revealed later, smiling. "He'd come home with some new toy we couldn't afford, and I'd find myself getting angry and upset—even though he'd spent his own money, from his own income, and we'd already agreed on how to handle our finances. I just couldn't cope with his big-spending ways. I'd find myself yelling at him."

"And I needed to forgive her for spoiling my fun," Steve adds, also with a smile on his face. "I had been all alone in making those decisions for a while. I wasn't used to being 'judged' for every purchase, having to explain my reasons for doing something. Where's the fun in that?"

Forgiving each other may need to be a daily practice, or it may be needed only when a major issue surfaces within the family. Either way, a couple's forgiving each other is crucial to the success and strength of their new relationship.

Even so, there's a huge difference between real forgiveness and denial. In the case of Ellen and Steve, it would not have been healthy for Ellen to simply stifle her natural response to Steve's impulse buying. And it would not have been wise for Steve to suppress his feelings when Ellen questioned his latest purchase or wanted some kind of explanation.

Ellen's reaction was a natural product of her experiences. Although she needed to learn how to respond properly, it was healthy for her to express her feelings to her new husband, whose behavior was also a natural product of his own history. Although he needed to learn to share decision-making and to seek more input from his wife, his choices expressed his personal values and beliefs. Forgiveness is not about suppressing our own identity.

Because they had approached the new relationship slowly with help from a trained counselor, Ellen and Steve were able to face their differences rationally. Without undue anger, without giving up on their remarriage, they worked on key issues in the counselor's office. They discovered that forgiving each other is a key strategy in forming a strong and lasting remarriage.

Forgiving Yourself

Perhaps the most difficult work is learning to forgive yourself. As we talk with divorced and remarried persons, one of the common themes that emerges is a sense of guilt or failure regarding the prior marriage. Post-divorce feelings of shame and personal failure are carried forward into the new relationship with the new partner.

Candy's husband left her with two very young children to raise. He filed for divorce immediately after leaving; when it was granted, he married his live-in girlfriend. He did not return to visit his children, and he did not answer calls, letters, or e-mails from Candy.

It was easier for her to forgive her ex-husband for leaving than it was for her to forgive herself. Long after he had remarried, Candy continued to feel personally responsible for the dissolution of the marriage.

"I had put on about 30 pounds since we were married, and I knew I didn't look as attractive or shapely as I had before," she comments. "Most of it happened with the two pregnancies. I'd gain weight for nine months, then have a lot of trouble trying to lose it again. After the divorce, I kept thinking that if I'd just kept myself in better shape, he wouldn't have left me."

She blamed herself over other issues as well. "With two children under four years old, I hadn't been able to keep the house looking clean and perfect all the time. I know he was frustrated and upset when the house didn't seem neat and tidy. He'd walk in the front door and start yelling about the kids' toys lying around, or their clothes lying around, or maybe the mess in the kitchen. He was always yelling about how the house looked.

"Even several years after our divorce, I kept wondering, *If I had kept the house neat and tidy, would he have stayed?* I'd feel really guilty about that, and I'd blame myself for not trying harder to keep him satisfied and happy."

Candy's response is typical of many divorced persons. Even when it might seem the other party was more "at fault," the abandoned partner can continue to struggle with mountains of internal guilt.

THIS CAN BE EQUALLY TRUE of the partner who did the leaving.

After nearly six years of being married, Justin walked out on his first family, which included two children, and never looked back. When his wife filed for divorce, he quickly consented. He had decided in his own mind that he and his wife were not compatible and that the relationship did not have a future.

He ran away from his wife, but couldn't escape his guilt. "For a couple of years I had trouble sleeping at night. I'd get sick easily, and I'd stay sick longer than usual. I didn't feel good physically, and I certainly didn't feel good emotionally. I didn't notice it at first, but I felt worse after I left my marriage than I felt while I was in it."

Then Justin attended a men's ministry event in a football stadium, invited by a close friend. Although he really didn't want to be there, he found himself enjoying the talks by prominent athletes and entertainment figures. By the end of the weekend, he was committing his life to Christ. This experience helped him begin to mature as a person.

"By the time I started to grow up," he admits, "my ex-wife had remarried and started a whole new family. She and her second husband had had two kids together by then, and they were raising my two kids as well. I couldn't exactly put things back the way they used to be—it was too late for that!"

He wrestled with intense feelings of guilt and shame, realizing he was primarily responsible for the end of the marriage, for the breakup of the family, and for whatever emotional struggles his children might be facing.

"I really believed that God had forgiven me," Justin says. "Somehow I understood that: God had truly wiped my record clean. But the hard thing was, how could I forgive myself? I had messed up—not in a small way, but in a way that affected three other people's lives, plus mine."

The church he had been attending had counselors on staff, and he began to meet with a mature, older Christian man weekly.

"He taught me how to forgive myself," Justin recalls. "It was slow and tough work, and sometimes I thought I wouldn't make it. Somehow, God helped me get through it. As I worked through the issues, I noticed I was sleeping a lot better at night, and I wasn't catching colds all the time like I had before. I was feeling better about life, smiling more often, recovering some of my old self."

The counselor specifically helped Justin in one particular way: "He showed me that no one deserves forgiveness, none of us do. That really helped me because I knew I didn't deserve to be forgiven. I knew my kids had a right to be mad at me the rest of their lives, and so did my ex-wife. I didn't deserve their mercy, their understanding, their forgiveness.

"It took a while, but slowly I realized that if everyone can be forgiven, then that applies to me, too. It doesn't apply to me because I deserve it; it just applies to me because I'm human."

He eventually remarried, becoming an instant father figure to three children whose biological dad had abandoned them. "I know I can't replace what they lost," he says now. "And I also know I can't love these kids enough to make up for the pain I've caused my own kids. I'm just trying to be the best dad I can, to be someone my new family can be really proud of."

Candy remarried also, after nearly five years as a single parent. "I still haven't taken the weight off," she laughs, "and the house is still a mess. But my new husband loves me just the way I am, and he loves the kids, too. Somehow I guess I've even managed to accept myself now, to be gentle to myself."

Forgive Again and Again

Whether we are forgiving others, forgiving a new spouse, or forgiving ourselves, one thing is sure: We'll need to keep on forgiving.

Those who have hurt us in the past may well keep hurting us in the present and on into the future. While we can and should protect ourselves physically, we may not be able to guard against the emotional pain others can cause. Our best hope is to forgive others—forgive them again—and keep on forgiving them.

While we are adjusting to a new relationship, we may be hurt by our new partner. His way of doing things may offend us. Her attitude may upset us. As we work toward understanding each other and building a strong remarriage, we'll need to keep on forgiving each other, keeping our lines of communication open.

As we recover from the wreckage of our past, we'll need to forgive our own

> **How Forgiveness Improves Your Remarriage Relationship**
>
> 1. Forgiving those who have hurt you in the past gives you less "baggage" to carry into your new relationship. You'll start the remarriage as a more balanced, more positive, more practical person if you are free from negative emotions like anger, resentment, and bitterness.
>
> 2. Forgiving each other is a necessary part of adjusting to your new relationship. As you sort out your personality styles and differences in attitudes and values, keep on forgiving each other. Find safety and shelter in the shared value of forgiveness.
>
> 3. Remember to forgive yourself, too. Nobody's perfect, and everyone struggles in the process of becoming mature. Since God has forgiven you, agree with God that you are now a forgiven person. Live in the freedom of His forgiveness.
>
> The Center for Marriage & Family Studies
> Del Mar, California

faults, mistakes, and failings. This may prove to be the most difficult forgiveness of all. But it is absolutely vital to our success and well-being.

"How many times?" Christ's disciples asked Him. "Should we forgive others seven times?" This seemed to them a very generous offer indeed. "No, not seven times," He responded in Matthew 18:22, "but seventy times seven." From His point of view, forgiveness was perpetual and ongoing. It was unlimited.

When we forgive others as Christ does, and when we keep on forgiving them according to His wise counsel, we build stronger and better relationships.

THEY DECLINE TO BE PROFILED for the book, insisting during a lengthy and laughter-filled conversation they shouldn't be role models. "After all," they both note, "we aren't perfect."

We smile, trying to explain that since there are no perfect people, there will never be a perfect marriage or a perfect remarriage. We explain we're not looking for perfection—we're just trying to cite examples of endurance!

They laugh at that, but still decline to be profiled.

"We aren't anything special," they declare.

Our search for long-term remarriages has brought us to this couple. It's now more than 40 years since they became husband and wife. It's apparent during the interview that their relationship is comfortable, their marriage intimate, their joy in life very much evident in their postretirement years.

SHE WAS BUSY RAISING A FAMILY when they met—her previous marriage had ended. There wasn't time for a typical dating relationship. She was too busy. Instead, he gradually began spending more time with her, and more time also with her young children.

It began as a good friendship.

They married, recalling now that her children were more confused than enthusiastic about the wedding. At the time, more than four decades ago, divorce and remarriage were far rarer in our culture.

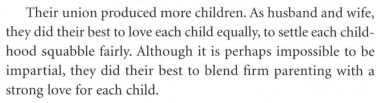
Their union produced more children. As husband and wife, they did their best to love each child equally, to settle each childhood squabble fairly. Although it is perhaps impossible to be impartial, they did their best to blend firm parenting with a strong love for each child.

That theme emerges several times in our conversation. "We did our best," they sigh, before sharing examples of problems and difficulties, setbacks and hardships. It seems most of their stories are about the hard times rather than the celebrations. "We tried," they often explain.

Looking on as observers 40 years after the fact, it's hard to understand why this couple is so modest about their achievements as a long-term remarried couple. From all available evidence, their union has been a success.

Surrounded by the laughter and play of grandchildren in this busy holiday season, they seem like prototypical grandparents. She bakes cookies in the kitchen while he lovingly admires a grandson's "new" car. Filling every room of the large house, the extended family has gathered for a lengthy holiday reunion. The pair cheerfully presides over the household—all the children are home.

One of their offspring is a missionary. One is a minister. The children are all involved in first marriages; none has divorced. The grandchildren, some of whom have reached marrying age, have done well in study and work environments.

"If you're not a success, who is?" we ask, trying to convince them.

"Well, you should profile people who have done it a lot better," they insist.

We make a final effort to insist that our book is not about perfection, not about finding superwoman and superman celebrating a super-remarriage.

Our efforts fail.

"We haven't done anything special," the couple demurs over coffee.

Forty years after remarrying, with two generations after them seeming well-grounded and reasonably healthy, this remarriage partnership still isn't ready to take credit for achievement or success.

"We're not role models for anything," they repeat.

"Oh yes, they are!" a nearby teenage granddaughter insists. We think she's right.

CHAPTER FIVE

Principle Number Four

Use Conflict to Get Better Acquainted

❀

*We always hope; and in all things it is better to hope
than to despair. When we return
to real trust in God, there will no longer
be room in our soul for fear.*

GOETHE

CONFLICT DOESN'T MEAN YOU'RE DEFECTIVE—it means you're normal.

The only way to avoid conflict completely is to retreat to a remote island and live alone! Even with that, some of us are neurotic enough that we'd manage to have plenty of conflict within ourselves.

Once there are two people in a relationship, there are two points of view, two sets of values, two personal histories, two ways of looking at the situation. As interaction develops and as decisions arise, it will become obvious that each person brings a unique and different mind-set to the relationship.

Uniqueness and difference are highly positive ingredients!

Early in a relationship, particularly during dating and courtship, it is often natural for one partner to withhold his or her opinion, for fear of causing a fight or an argument to take place. It's possible for this stage of the relationship to carry forward all the way up to the wedding day. It's very unusual, however, for the stage to last much beyond that. And besides being rare, it's actually an unhealthy pattern for relating to each other.

As WE WORKED WITH BOB AND DEBBIE, both insisted they'd never had a fight in the first three years of their remarriage. We were impressed and amazed, but we kept listening.

What we all discovered together was that, in the first three years of their marriage, Debbie had never voiced a strong opinion. As strange as that seems, she was very content to let Bob make the choices, Bob weigh the decisions, Bob set the tone for the whole household.

The result, on the surface, was a relationship that was smooth and simple, free of fighting and devoid of arguments. Yet beneath the surface, Debbie often disagreed with Bob's opinions and choices. Eventually she began exploding, seemingly for no reason, and was he ever surprised! They weren't talking with us because their relationship was still smooth—they were seeking our advice because major conflict had been erupting.

It was about time! Often we avoid conflict, believing it reveals something negative or harmful about ourselves or our relationship. We see disagreement as a sign of weakness or imperfection, deciding that superficial harmony and unity mean all is well.

In reality, harmony on the surface may mean that important areas of disagreement are not being discovered, discussed, and resolved. Unity on the surface may be a shallow substitute for the hard work of getting acquainted.

Conflict Means It's Time to Get Better Acquainted

Remarried couples are highly likely to be attracted to each other due to common interests and common experiences. Shared realities like suffering through a messy divorce, struggling to raise children as a single parent, and striving to make ends meet on a limited budget are unifying experiences that often provide a basis for mutual attraction and eventual remarriage.

In the courtship phase, differences of perspective may be minimized, whether intentionally or simply unconsciously. It's normal to present ourselves in the best possible light—as more relaxed, more humorous, and more "together" than we actually are. After all, isn't that what courtship is really about? How else can we attract a mate?

For this reason alone, a lengthy period of dating is highly valuable for persons considering a remarriage. The longer the period of friendship and getting acquainted, the more likely it is that the "true self" will emerge in each person. The relationship will begin on a much stronger basis if it is a planned merger of one true self with another true self, rather than a done-on-a-whim pairing of imaginary, romanticized images.

True love requires the presence of true selves.

Wanda and Rick were discouraged by the fact they fought almost constantly for the first year of their remarriage. It wasn't hand-to-hand combat; rather, it was a steady stream of bickering, arguing, and disagreeing.

Through it all, they stayed committed to each other. There was no discussion or threat of ending the relationship. However, common courtesy was often thrown out the window: Arguments were arguments, plain and simple.

A year or so into their remarriage they requested an assessment from a trained marriage counselor. To their surprise, the "state of their union" was much healthier than they expected or believed.

What had happened was this: In the midst of the bickering, each partner had done a great deal of self-disclosure. Thanks to the high volume and frequent expression, each partner had developed an accurate understanding of the perspectives, values, and opinions of the other.

The result? Wanda and Rick were well-acquainted. They knew each other. Their compatibility quotients were high and healthy, and the counselor's eventual prognosis for them was largely positive.

Should you bicker your way into getting acquainted? Probably not. Yet the fact remains that the more frequently you express a true opinion, rather than withholding or stifling your true response, the better the chance your partner will learn who you really are. Similarly, as your partner expresses feelings and values, you'll learn more about your partner.

Conflict is an opportunity to get better acquainted, a chance to learn something about the background, history, experiences, or beliefs of the person you've married. Rather than burying or avoiding conflict, bringing it to the light allows a couple to learn about each other, serve and encourage each other, and grow closer and deeper in their relationship.

If this seems to be an idealized view of conflict, it isn't. Rather, it's an intentional paradigm shift. Instead of viewing conflict as an enemy to be feared and avoided, remarried couples need to learn to welcome conflict as a friend.

How you think about conflict, how you feel about it, is critically important to the success of your relationship. Having a positive attitude about conflict is crucial to that eventual success.

Conflict is ready to help you. It is a teacher. The presence of disagreement means it's time to go back to class, watch the Powerpoint slides, and learn a new lesson. Do you think you already know it all? You don't! Thinking about conflict as an educational tool will help you disarm any irrational fear of disagreeing.

Once we learn to welcome conflict rather than fearing it, we can learn about each other—and we can also learn a lot more about ourselves. Remarriage, like any close relationship, functions as a great "mirror" in revealing to us our true identity. But if conflict is to be positive in its outcome, it needs to be managed and approached in a positive way.

Learning to Disagree…Agreeably

Have you ever encountered married couples that agree with each other about almost everything? What's up with that? Perhaps one partner is delusional.

If you measure a relationship by the amount of agreement—or by the lack of any disagreement—you're using the wrong standard. Agreement is an eventual outcome of lengthy and healthy marriages, yet just as commonly a lasting and healthy marriage contains mutually acceptable disagreements.

Healthy married couples disagree about many things, but they've learned how to approach those disagreements. They've learned which ones to resolve and which ones to respectfully leave unresolved. They've learned the crucial value of timing in the successful resolution of expressed differences.

A healthy remarriage can contain a substantial amount of disagreement, yet still produce a close, affectionate, growing relationship. Unity is not a result of identical opinions; it is a result of showing respect for the opinions of others. This becomes more possible as couples learn how to disagree...agreeably.

The following guidelines highlight six of the most important issues for you to consider in learning how to disagree agreeably.

Guideline #1: Not While You're Hot

Timing is everything.

The first two guidelines for learning to disagree agreeably involve choosing your time wisely. Conflict can emerge at any time, but it should not necessarily be dealt with when it emerges. Sometimes, the moment of conflict is the *worst possible time* to address areas of disagreement. It may actually make matters worse—by causing a small issue to escalate into a larger argument or fight.

One key in knowing when to tackle conflict is being aware of your current emotional state. Are you angry and upset? If so, this is not a strategic time to begin working on solving the disagreement.

Simply put, the time to resolve conflict is "not while you're hot." "People with a hot temper do foolish things," the writer of Proverbs observes, but "wiser people remain calm" (Proverbs 14:17).

People who are angry tend to say and do things that exaggerate or distort how they truly feel. Unfortunately, those around them are not skilled in interpreting the difference between feelings and actions, or between feelings and words. Consequently, those taking the brunt of anger tend to feel unloved, disrespected, and possibly even unsafe. It can take a long time to repair the damage caused by a few moments of careless speech while angry.

If you are very quick to become angry, you should seek professional help on your own—without involving your remarriage partner. The issues that trigger the anger within you are deeper than—and almost certainly predate—your current relationship with your spouse. Learning how to address your anger will be one of the most meaningful gifts you can ever give to your mate.

If your anger is sudden and fleeting, flaring up in response to specific trigger events, stay away from discussions and conversations with your spouse while you're angry. Instead of resolving conflict, your anger may well make it worse, increasing the number of issues on the table or deepening the sense of insult or offense your partner is experiencing.

It's a watchword worth repeating: "not while you're hot." Wait until you've cooled down. Then, without involving your partner yet, take a good long look at the situation in which you became angry. Try to learn from it and discover what the "trigger" was.

Mark frequently lashed out in anger against Charlotte, his second wife. While angry, he'd begin to lecture her about how and why she needed to change. Do you think she was listening? Do you think he had found her "teachable moment"?

Gradually, with help from a skilled counselor, he identified several situations that were trigger events for him. One of them, one which led to frequent outbursts from him and frequent conflicts with Charlotte, involved the condition and appearance of the kitchen. For whatever reason, Mark believed a clean kitchen was vital. When he came home from a day at the office and found cereal spilled on the floor, milk puddled on the counter, and debris pretty much everywhere, he'd begin to yell at his wife, their children, and anyone else who might be home at the time.

Suffice it to say those moments were not an ideal time to begin resolving areas of disagreement. His family learned to avoid him when he was angry.

Mark began to notice his anger and the kinds of situations that tended to trigger his unreasonable outbursts. Concurrently, Charlotte wisely began to make a special effort to clean up the kitchen before he got home.

Meanwhile, in the office of a counselor, away from the kitchen and far removed from the emotion of the incident, Mark and Charlotte began to learn how to talk to each other with respect and listen to each other attentively. With the anger gone, Charlotte found it was safe to approach her husband with requests for change. With his perspective unclouded by a rush of emotion, he found it easier to listen to his wife and appreciate her point of view.

Many areas of disagreement can be resolved directly by a couple, without any need for counseling. And learning to have discussions "away from the heat of battle" is vitally important to success. If one of you is angry and wishes to resolve a conflict, the other should politely, respectfully, but firmly insist on waiting until the anger has passed. It is much more effective to resolve disagreements when emotions are calmer.

Guideline #2: Within Reason, Wait Until *Both* of You Are Ready

It is often said that newly married couples tend to have sex when either one of them is ready; couples married for a longer term tend to have sex when *both* of them are "in the mood."

When it comes to resolving conflict and discussing areas of disagreement, it's extremely wise to wait until both of you are ready and willing to talk. Yet it should also be noted that some personality types would prefer to *never* discuss a problem. Waiting for them to be ready would involve waiting forever.

Both partners in a remarriage need to be willing to have clear, specific conversations about areas of disagreement or conflict. Neither should have to force the issue, nagging until the spouse consents to have a discussion. If a discussion is birthed by nagging, its chances of success are small at best.

If both are willing to have such discussions, then the issue is finding a time at which both partners can pay attention, be open to learning, and show respect for other points of view. There will probably not be an ideal time of day, an ideal room of the house, or an ideal moment to have such discussions. Rather, finding a useful time will be a matter of compromise and acceptance.

Turning off the television, putting the kids to bed early, canceling an event on the schedule, and other such proactive measures may be required in order to create the kind of time you'll need to have a positive discussion. Do what it takes. After all, VCRs, TiVo, and similar devices make it possible to do that "must-see" viewing later.

Again, don't insist on waiting for "ideal" conditions for a discussion. Real life conspires against every meaningful attempt at positive change, whether it's taking on a new discipline, trying to grow spiritually, or getting yourself in better shape physically. But learning to have healthy and positive discussions with your spouse is well worth the effort.

If you choose your time wisely, a discussion is much less likely to feel like a fight, and much more likely to feel like a meaningful conversation. You may be tired, you may be emotionally worn out, you may have had a long day—but if you begin to make time for resolving disagreement in a healthy way, you'll learn that the rewards far outweigh the necessary sacrifices.

You are very likely to end up moving toward common ground as time passes and your discussions mature. Yet even if you continue to disagree, you'll be finding healthy and positive ways to allow disagreement to exist within the context of a stable, committed, loving relationship.

With issues of timing addressed, let's turn to *how* you discuss problems.

Guideline #3: Express Yourself Without Attacking

Other drivers are crazy.

This is a fact of life in Southern California, where each driver behaves as if the freeway exists only for him or her and no other drivers could possibly be sharing it. This point of view makes it unnecessary, for example, to look in your rearview mirror before changing lanes. Since you're the only driver on the road, why bother with mirrors?

Karen and Chaz fought about driving on a regular basis. They didn't fight when she was the driver and he was the passenger. Their arguments erupted only when Chaz drove with Karen in the passenger seat.

"I'd be fingering my prayer beads all the way to work." Karen laughs, which she can do today because the couple has learned how to resolve conflict in ways that are healthy and positive. Yet for a while, riding in the car with her husband at the wheel almost always produced an argument or fight.

"I do tend to drive aggressively," Chaz admits. "I have a schedule to keep, and I drive to get where I'm going, not to stop and smell the roses."

"You run right over the roses!" Karen inserts.

They both laugh—a healthy change from past patterns.

EARLY IN THEIR REMARRIAGE, THOUGH, the issue of driving was a hot topic.

"You're driving like an idiot!" Karen would yell at Chaz during their morning commute along the I-5 freeway. "You're going to get us both killed!"

Needless to say, this was not a teachable moment for her husband.

"Have I ever wrecked the car yet?" he'd yell back. "It's a lot safer to drive aggressively than it is to just let everybody else hog in. You have no idea how many accidents I've avoided by driving like this."

"Well, slow down!" Karen would insist.

He, of course, would accelerate in response.

Although they can laugh about it now, at the time it wasn't funny. The couple didn't seek counseling, didn't take time to read a helpful book, and didn't practice techniques of ideal communication in order to resolve their area of disagreement. Instead, they sat down one Saturday morning—a day that didn't involve any commuting—and had the fight of their lives.

"Where do you get off calling me an unsafe driver?" Chaz began. "What gives you the right to accuse me of that? Would you like to see my driving record? It's perfect—I've never had a wreck, never gotten a ticket!"

It was an "aha" moment for Karen. She suddenly realized she'd been wounding her husband's ego by implying he was an unsafe, unskilled, reckless driver. Remarkably, she realized she'd been approaching the problem in an unhelpful way. She freely admits to venting a lot of anger during this particular fight, but she gradually realized she needed to change the way she dealt with things. Before the fight ended she had changed her tone considerably. It worked like a charm.

"You *are* a safe driver," she eventually said. "I apologize for all the names I've been calling you and all the things I've said. Will you forgive me?"

Amazingly, Chaz did.

"Here's the thing," Karen continued. "Riding over there in the passenger seat, it scares me to death when we get so close to other cars—the ones right beside my window, the ones in front of us—all of them.

"In my rational mind, I know you're not going to hit those cars, but in the moment—help!—I get really scared. My whole body reacts with fear because it seems like we're about to have an accident. I know we're not going to have one, but my fear is just automatic!"

Perhaps because the fight had exhausted them both by that point, Chaz was actually listening. For once, without feeling attacked about his skills as a driver, he was open to learning. (Chaz the driver was a legend in his own mind.)

"That makes sense," he admitted. "I can see how that would scare you. It freaks me out to ride with Fred at work, just going to lunch. He bobs and weaves like a madman, and I always think we're about to wreck."

Karen nodded. In that moment, there was the beginning of an understanding. From that moment on, there was a change in the way the two of them related while driving.

Were things immediately perfect? Of course not. But they were different, and in this case different was good. Chaz, while driving with his wife on board, has learned to temper his aggressive driving by allowing more visible space between and around other cars. He is still an aggressive driver, but he respects his spouse's feelings and has dramatically altered his approach to the morning commute.

Karen, for her part, has quit insisting that a crash is imminent. Although her body still sometimes tenses up in response to her husband's driving, she has learned not to lash out at him with insults and anger. She has also taken note that so far he has an unblemished record on the roadway.

"He's a very good driver, actually," she says with a grin, "although I really hate to admit that. He hasn't wrecked our car yet..."

"And she's so much better as a front-seat passenger than my mom is," Chaz comments with a laugh. "My mom just closes her eyes. I can see her lips move, though I can't always hear the words of her prayers."

Focusing and Becoming Aware

Chaz and Karen went from yelling to laughing because they learned how to express their feelings without attacking the virtue, skill, or identity of their mate. Each became aware of the other's perspective. Each made some changes.

Respect for your partner's identity and maturity are highly important. Instead of asking a question like "Why are you always such an idiot?" try using an approach like "Here's how I feel when this is happening."

Be very specific, and focus on exactly how you feel in a given situation. When you express your feelings without attacking your partner's identity, your partner may feel safe enough to actually listen—and concede the virtue and importance of your opinions. Rarely does anyone listen while being yelled at—you'll discover a loving partner will usually listen when you express how you feel in a clear, specific, nonthreatening way.

When talking about an area of disagreement, focus on your own feelings. Express yourself in sentences such as "This is how I feel when…" rather than completing a sentence in a way that attacks your partner. ("This is how I feel when you drive like an idiot" is not a useful approach, since it ends with an attack.)

It may take a while, but strive to become aware of the ways your words attack or tear down your partner's worth, skill, or values. Stifle those kinds of words and phrases. If you slip up and say the wrong thing—and you will—apologize quickly and restate the comment in a new way. Over time, you'll learn to get it right the first time. You'll discover a new way of speaking.

When we express ourselves without attacking the other person, we make it much less likely that the other person will respond with defensiveness and anger. We make it much more possible for the other person to help us learn and grow.

Guideline #4: Explain Yourself Without Defending Yourself

"I am *not* being defensive!" Doug's voice boomed from the kitchen. There was a moment of silence, then his laughter echoed down the hall. "Um, well, maybe I guess I am," he went on sheepishly.

His honest admission to Cathy, his wife, broke the tension of the moment.

When we believe we are being attacked, one of our most natural reactions is to defend ourselves. We lash out at the source of the attack, raging against the unfair accusation, the injustice being done against us, and so on.

Some of us become defensive very easily. When we're driving, a simple question like "Why are you turning left?" can sound like an accusation to our overdefensive ears. Somehow we hear, *Don't you know where you're going? You're turning the wrong way!* even though this is not what our partner said or meant.

If you are married to an overdefensive person, the preceding guideline—about expressing yourself without attacking—is of vital importance in communicating with your spouse. You'll need to reread that section every now and then. You'll need to learn how to change your way of expressing things so you don't somehow appear to be attacking your partner.

Further, both parties in a remarriage need to learn how to explain themselves without becoming defensive. This vital communication skill helps keep a potential fight from escalating into all-out war.

It takes two to fight, or at least to sustain a fight. When one person attacks, the fight won't get very far unless a defensive reaction occurs. As we learn how to control our emotions and avoid being defensive, we are actually learning how to prevent many fights, and how to quickly limit many emotional tirades.

Cathy and Doug were learning about defensiveness when Doug had his "aha" moment in the kitchen. They had driven home from work together. There was a church event scheduled for the evening and Doug had volunteered to cook, to which Cathy had swiftly agreed.

A few minutes later, from another room of the house, she had yelled to her husband, "Hey, is dinner about ready?" His ears had heard that question as, *What's taking so long?* So he'd gotten defensive, yelling back, "I'm cooking as fast as I can!"

Cathy, having recently learned in this area, called back in a somewhat sweeter tone of voice, "You're being defensive right now, honey!"

To this, Doug, as we saw earlier, first yelled back that he wasn't being defensive—then noticed he actually was.

Noticing Your Emotions—the First Step

When your spouse asks a question or makes a statement, do you feel like you are being personally challenged in some way? Do your ears manage to hear a complaint buried somewhere within the question? If so, you may be struggling with defense mechanisms that prevent you from understanding yourself and your partner. You'll need to learn the same lessons that helped Cathy and Doug reduce their fighting considerably.

It was a major and healthy sign of progress when Doug caught himself in the act of being defensive, and was able to laugh about it instead of lashing out further. In the story above, Cathy was not even remotely complaining about the speed of her husband's cooking. Instead, in the midst of changing clothes, putting on makeup, and getting ready for church she just wanted to know when dinner would be served.

Doug, though, with his defense mechanisms at the ready, managed to feel like his wife was attacking the speed of his food preparation. Instead of cheerfully calling back "About ten minutes, honey!" he yelled, "I'm cooking as fast as I can!"—a clear indication of a defensive reaction.

Do you recognize yourself or your mate in this example? If so, you'll need to learn about disarming the defense mechanisms that cause us to strike back instead of responding calmly and clearly.

Start to practice becoming aware of your emotions and attitudes. Doug, busy in the kitchen making dinner, was already worrying about the time and wondering if he'd taken on more than he could achieve. Emotionally, he was feeling stressed about that, stressed from cooking, and was still stressed from a tough day at the office. (This does not excuse his defensiveness—it merely explains it.)

Doug managed to hear a simple question as a barbed complaint. Only when Cathy caught him in the act of being defensive did Doug realize his own emotions. To his credit, he noticed what he was doing and changed his tone.

Waiting a Moment—the Second Step

In addition to becoming aware of your emotions, practice waiting a moment before responding to questions or comments. In that moment, think about what's been said and try to frame an emotion-free answer.

We sometimes suggest visualization exercises to help in this process. To Doug, we might suggest visualizing that the question "Hey, is dinner about ready?" had been asked not by his wife, but by the cute little redheaded four-year-old neighbor girl who was playing in the kitchen with his four-year-old son.

Would Doug have snapped back angrily at the little girl's inquiry, "Hey, I'm cooking as fast as I can!"? Of course not. He would have to be an awfully rude person to vent his anger at a neighbor girl who was asking him a simple question. Yet Doug had no hesitation at all yelling a retort to his wife.

What does this truth tell us about our defense mechanisms? For one thing, we learn that how we respond to verbal input can depend on who we are talking to. In some cases we force ourselves to be more tolerant, more quiet, more polite, and more sociable than we might otherwise feel like being. Since we know how to do this around little children, for example, it's not too big a step to start applying this same tolerance to the partner under our roof! We typically make this effort if we have guests over for dinner, if the minister has dropped by for a visit, or if our partner's parents or children are in the same room. Although frustrated and perhaps angry, we stop and frame our response in a way that is socially acceptable. We respond with kindness.

If we're willing to do this in a public situation to protect our own reputation and keep up appearances, then we can learn to do this in private situations in order to honor our spouse and learn to communicate wisely.

Love is willing to learn, willing to change, and willing to behave better in its quest for a deeper, fuller, more satisfying marriage relationship.

Guideline #5: Listen More, Speak Less

Forty minutes into our first counseling session with Joyce and Clarence, we still hadn't heard Joyce complete a sentence. We had asked her a number of very direct questions, only to have Clarence interject a response before she could finish.

"She doesn't agree with that," he opined at one point. Remarried less than a year, he was already speaking for his new wife as if he knew her thoroughly and was an expert on her opinions and beliefs.

Later in the session, he offered, "That's not how she would do that. She has a completely different approach to that whole thing."

Eventually we smiled at Clarence and asked him to stop speaking out. Then we asked Joyce the same questions we had asked previously. Not surprising to us, her answers were much different than the ones her husband had supplied when he was supposedly speaking on her behalf. Some of the time, in fact, her answers were the exact opposite of what he had predicted.

Over the course of several sessions together—and as revealed on written questionnaires the couple filled out separately, we found this new husband didn't know his wife nearly as well as he thought he did.

The reason for his ignorance was simple: It's hard to get to know a person when you're the one doing all the talking.

The Pathway to Understanding

It's natural for opposite personalities to be attracted to each other; it's not uncommon for one partner to be more sociable, more outgoing, more extroverted, and more talkative than the other, especially in public. There's nothing wrong with that pattern, nothing that needs to be changed in order for the couple to have a positive and healthy relationship. However, if the couple is ever going to get deeply acquainted and mutually attached, their private reality will need to include verbalization by both of them.

The skill of listening is crucial to learning. Clarence, for example, truly believed he knew his wife. But her answers on the questionnaire shocked him in some cases. He apparently mistook her silence—while he talked on and on—to mean she was in complete agreement with his views. He should have taken a clue from her politics: In the previous election the two had voted for different political parties and candidates.

Clarence had missed many opportunities to get better acquainted with his new wife. He had talked right through those moments, not stopping to listen. This demonstrates that the pathway to deeper understanding runs directly through your ears. Quietly listening to your partner's point of view, without interrupting or telling stories of your own, is one of the most powerful and effective ways to become acquainted with each other at a deep level.

Taking time to listen should be a high priority in your relationship. Although it's wonderful to have "date nights" and perhaps attend a new movie, the danger is this—it's possible to sit in silence all the way through a feature film, then go home without knowing each other any better than you did before.

Over dinner, in front of a roaring fire, sitting outdoors on your patio, or simply driving across town to a shared appointment, take advantage of any opportunity you have to get better acquainted by listening. Ask questions about topics you know are interesting to your partner. Instead of interrupting and sharing your own experiences, make a conscious effort to keep listening.

Follow-up questions that relate specifically to something your partner has just said can be effective in learning who they are. The practice of "reflective listening" involves interacting with what you are hearing by asking further questions, then patiently waiting for answers to emerge.

Over time, Clarence learned to talk a bit less. Joyce learned to speak up a bit more. Their conversational interaction became more balanced and mutual. Also over time, he began to learn his wife's values, priorities, and history. His learning increased greatly as he discovered that by keeping his mouth shut he was gaining lots of information about his spouse.

As you've no doubt heard before, God gave each of us two ears and only one mouth. That's a clue. Start to practice listening more than you speak, and you may be surprised at how much you can learn.

Guideline #6: Value What You Hear

Elaine thought her husband was listening to her. After all, he nodded his head thoughtfully and gave her occasional verbal feedback. He seemed to be fully present for their conversations at the dinner table or in the living room. Yet only five minutes later, when Elaine would mention something they had just discussed, Jack would have no idea what she was talking about.

Her husband had mastered the art of seeming to pay attention while in reality ignoring the conversation. Although she felt valued in the moment, Elaine ended up feeling neglected and ignored once she realized Jack had only feigned interest.

Paying attention to someone by listening carefully is only half the issue. The second half of the same issue involves valuing what you learn as you listen.

Few things are more frustrating than expressing an idea, opinion, or experience, only to have your partner forget about it a few seconds later. This pattern has the effect of reducing communication over time, and it explains in part why some married couples gradually drift into separate lives.

Value the Topic, Value the Person

While you may not have a strong natural interest in the topics of your partner's conversation, it pays to develop an attentive concern. Valuing what you hear shows that you value the person you are hearing it from.

Denise had no natural interest in cars or mechanical things, but when she married for the second time, her husband, Jason, was a part-time racer and full-time auto enthusiast. She began by merely *seeming* to pay attention to cars—then she realized she needed to actually learn what Jason was talking about.

By attending races with her new husband, chatting with other spouses at car rallies and auto shows, and doing some reading, she began to build a knowledge base in a subject in which she had had no prior interest whatsoever. Within a few years of marrying Jason, she could participate meaningfully in conversations with her husband about short-block engines, gear ratios, and superchargers.

Denise would never have learned these things on her own. She made a conscious decision to pay attention to Jason's hobbies, even when the topics of his conversation held little natural interest for her. Further into the relationship, she made a conscious decision to learn about this favored pursuit of his in order to get to know him better and to share a common interest.

She never read a book telling her to do these things. Yet her behavior sent her new husband a clear message. By listening attentively, retaining what she was learning, and developing an interest in a new subject, she let Jason know she highly valued and respected him as a person.

"We're so much closer together now that we have racing in common," Denise relates. "Who knew? At first I really didn't care about it at all."

For Robert, who remarried later in life, it meant learning about quilts, quilting, and quilters. His third wife, an accomplished quilter, traveled to shows and sales throughout the Ozarks and south-central United States.

Robert was ignorant of the quilting world and would have happily remained so. However, he wisely realized that quilting

Learning to Disagree...Agreeably

In summary, here are the six guidelines for resolving your conflicts:

1. **Not while you're hot.** In a moment of anger, you're likely to say things you don't mean or exaggerate your feelings.

2. **Wait until you're both ready to talk.** There may not be an "ideal" moment; be willing to compromise on scheduling.

3. **Express yourself without attacking.** Avoid using words that threaten or demean your partner. Instead, talk gently about your feelings, speaking clearly and specifically.

4. **Explain yourself without defending.** Learn to notice your emotions. Most of us manage to behave politely around children and guests—apply the same self-control when dealing with your partner. Speak without hostility; react without bristling.

5. **Listen more than you speak.** There's no substitute for really listening to your partner—asking questions rather than telling your own stories and voicing your own opinions.

6. **Value what you hear.** Seeming to listen is not enough. Listen well enough to learn about what you're hearing. You may even develop a new interest or hobby—something that you and your partner can enjoy together.

The Center for Marriage & Family Studies
Del Mar, California

was a major passion of his wife's life, so he should learn at least a little something about it.

Six months later, he was making his first quilt—at 62 years old. The project involved swatches of old sweatshirts and T-shirts Robert had worn throughout his life. Cutting the shirts into squares, learning how to apply backing, and sewing the pieces into a finished quilt gave him a new pride.

"Just don't tell any of my buddies about this!" he begs, though, rolling his eyes. "There goes my macho image!"

Although Robert is unlikely to become a full-time quilter, he sent his wife a strong and positive message by becoming involved in her craft. His actions told his wife he valued her as a person and as a partner.

"At first, when she'd talk about quilting, my eyes would glaze over," he recalls. "I had no idea what she was talking about, and I didn't care. Now, when she gets going on some topic about quilting, I usually at least understand what she's talking about. I guess that you really can teach an old dog some new tricks after all!"

Part Two

Strategies for Building Your Remarriage Relationship

CHAPTER SIX

Your First Choices

Strategies for the First Few Steps

❋

Starting over takes courage and hope:
   courage to face your fears and move forward,
      hope to help you believe in your possibilities.
Be courageous and hopeful:
   face the sunrise rather than the sunset.

A S A READER OF THIS BOOK, you may have long since "taken the first few steps" by getting remarried. Feel free to skip ahead and look at strategies for some of the tougher challenges you may already be facing.

If, however, you are at an early stage along your remarriage pathway, or if you are just contemplating remarriage, the topics we discuss here can get your new relationship—and if applicable, your new family—off to a strong and positive start.

Let's look at several of the crucial issues involved in starting over.

About the Wedding

As Cheryl Mayfield Brown and husband Bill Brown discovered when they were planning their wedding—the second for them both—the wedding-planning culture is focused primarily on first marriages. The couple met resistance and questions as they sought to arrange an elaborate, romantic second wedding. The mind-set among wedding planners seemed to be, "You've already had *one* elaborate wedding—why make such a fuss the *second* time?"*

But remarriages are booming, and an increasing number of remarrying couples are choosing a fully staged, beautiful wedding. Even those whose plans are less grand may still seek out a wedding planner for good counsel about legal, financial, or other remarriage issues.

Katie has regrets. "I was married by a justice of the peace the first time. The ceremony was over in about five minutes. There was no music, there were only two witnesses, and the whole experience was depressing. I was so focused on just getting married that I gave up my hopes of having a nice wedding."

Katie's experience is hardly unique. Contrary to the mind-set of most wedding planners, many couples got married originally in circumstances that were anything but romantic, fancy, or flowery. When it comes to the second trip down the aisle, some of those couples are choosing to have the celebration they always wanted but didn't previously have.

"People are still a little bit ashamed about getting married again," Doug says with a rueful smile. "There's still a stigma to it, in some ways. That's why Celia and I wanted a big wedding, in a church, with all the trappings. We wanted to show people we're not ashamed of our love for each other, we're not ashamed of our marriage. We're just starting over, that's all—and we're trying to do it right this time!"

Diverse Views

As might be expected, church policies can vary. The Christian community is not of one mind regarding second marriages,

---

* Out of their own experience, Cheryl and Bill eventually founded what has become a thriving and successful business: Twice Is Nice Encore Bridal Creations in Charlotte, North Carolina. From simply offering wedding-day advice to "full service," the Browns have established a business model that caters specifically to couples that are remarrying. And the business that began as a secondary pursuit has quickly become a primary occupation for them!

with theological views ranging from "not ever, not for any reason" to "by the grace of God, let's help you have a wonderful marriage this time."

Chatting with remarried couples reveals a diversity of opinions about the significance of the wedding day in the overall process. Doug and Celia wanted to invite their friends and family to a joyous, festive, all-the-trappings ceremony. Richard and Kassie, on the other hand, got remarried quietly and inexpensively, sending announcements after the fact to a small number of friends.

The approach you take to the wedding ceremony may reveal your overall attitude about getting married again. If you are hesitant to proclaim your remarriage, you may be dealing with issues of guilt or shame on at least some level. Premarriage counseling, which we'll discuss later, can be of high value to you in sorting out your thoughts and feelings.

GOOD REASONS FOR MAKING the wedding a priority can include

- producing happy and joyous memories for the children
- having an opportunity to register for and receive gifts from a wide circle of friends and family
- establishing from the beginning that you are seeking God's blessing and presence in the marriage relationship

Each of these priorities might lead to making the wedding a significant event in your remarriage journey.

"We wanted a church ceremony because we wanted to honor God this time," Carl reports. "Both of us had been involved in marriages that didn't honor God, and that didn't establish Jesus Christ as the center of the home and family. This time, we wanted to get it right from the very beginning.

"We were blessed to find a minister who was very supportive

of us, one who administered personality tests, talked us through our history as divorced persons, and really helped our relationship with God and with each other grow deeper.

"By the time our wedding day rolled around, we were ready to stand in the front of the chapel, praise God, and seek His blessing on this new union. We had a lengthy time of contemporary worship incorporated into our ceremony. And that became, for us, one of the best parts of the whole wedding day!"

Carl's wife, Jackie, immediately agrees with him. "The sense of God's presence, as we started our new life together, was very tangible. Instead of the guilt we felt for having been such failures in the past, our wedding day was about living in God's grace."

As discussed in the example which opened this book, many remarried couples intentionally spotlight their children in the wedding ceremony. A bride in a second marriage is often escorted down the aisle by a grown son, or perhaps a much-loved son-in-law. A number of such brides have chosen to walk the aisle escorted by *all* of their children, highlighting the fact that it is the children, rather than the bride's parents, who are "giving her away" this time.

On the other side, good reasons for downplaying the wedding ceremony might include

- the ever-present financial challenges faced by couples getting remarried
- a conscious choice to use the available money in other ways, instead of spending it on flowers, cake, invitations, gowns, and other flourishes

Some couples believe it's inappropriate to solicit—or to appear to solicit—gifts for a second wedding day. "It was only eight years since I was first married," Shawna explains, "and I was still using the wedding gifts. It didn't seem right to ask people to get me gifts again. It seemed tacky. So we had a very simple wedding, announced it later, and put 'no gifts, please' on all the announcements we sent out."

So did the couple receive gifts anyway?

"Yes, we did." Shawna laughs. "Actually, quite a few people ended up sending us gifts, including some very nice things. So maybe regardless of how we feel about it, other people *want to* give gifts and are happy to have the chance."

About the Honeymoon

As is true of first marriages, opinions vary on the importance and value of a honeymoon in the process of becoming one as a couple in a second marriage.

Jim and Jessica are "true believers" in a honeymoon's high priority. "We took a seven-day cruise to Alaska," Jessica beams. "It was such a wonderful, romantic way to begin our marriage. It was just the two of us, with great food, great scenery, great entertainment. Neither of us had been on a cruise before, but both of us had always wanted to.

"Jim and I just concentrated on being together, being in love, and forming our new union. Both of us gained about five pounds that week"—she laughs—"but frankly we gained so much more. We established our new relationship in a way that just wouldn't have happened if we hadn't decided to get away and be all by ourselves."

Experts agree. Making the honeymoon a priority, even if you're a remarried couple with children, helps establish your husband-wife relationship as valued and as a primary unifying factor in your new household. Because your children need to have a sense of security and safety within the new family relationship, a honeymoon is one way to send them the message that their parents love each other—a message that may visibly contrast with their prior experience.

In summary, good reasons for making the honeymoon a priority may include

- having time to bond together as a new couple, away from the stresses and pressures of everyday life

- sending a message to the children that the new couple is deeply attached and committed to a united future
- simply celebrating the joy of finding each other and making a fresh start

Even if the "honeymoon" is just a night or two away together, it can still be useful in establishing the priorities of your new family. In the long journey of a successful remarriage, carving out time for romance and bonding will need to be an ongoing priority for you. Rooting that priority in the earliest decisions of the new union can help send the right message—right from the start.

The key in planning a successful honeymoon is not about high expense, but rather about *high privacy* and *high impact*. Separating from the pressure and expectations of everyday life can help a couple relax, unwind, and unite.

It's not uncommon for one partner, typically the husband, to play the role of honeymoon planner, sometimes even keeping the details secret until the honeymoon actually happens. Particularly in a remarriage context, though, it is probably wiser to plan a honeymoon mutually rather than singly. Each partner should contribute true feelings, true values, and true desires as the concept of the honeymoon takes shape. The choice to have a honeymoon, and the type of honeymoon to have, should be a shared value rather than an imposed one.

Reasons for downplaying the honeymoon might include

- financial stress
- the presence of infants or very young children in the new household
- the need to wait till vacation time or family leave might be available from an employer

Still another possibility is the idea of involving the children in the honeymoon, a choice that is growing in popularity among couples choosing to remarry.

Consider a "Familymoon"

As with much of the terminology for remarriage, the term "familymoon" falls short. However, it does manage to convey the core idea: taking the newly blended family along on the remarried couple's honeymoon experience.

One cruise-ship line, for instance, offers a stateroom with separate areas for the couple and the children. A Caribbean resort offers a "second honeymoon" package that includes babysitting services; remarried families are housed in two-bedroom villas so that parents can have the privacy they seek, yet still be near their children during their tropical vacation. Another such resort includes a wedding in the package deal, as do some other providers.

Less affluent families are finding their own ways to make similar choices, often utilizing all-suite hotels or similar apartment-style properties. Built as extended-stay dwellings for business travelers, they generally furnish most of the amenities of home, such as kitchens, while also providing exercise rooms, pools, and spas, as well as easy access to nearby restaurants and malls.*

KEN AND MADELYN TOOK their three children, her two and his one, on a weeklong honeymoon to California, staying in hotel suites in two locations. All three children were under age nine, and all shared a living-room space with a foldout sofa bed while the parents occupied a bedroom—behind a closed door yet still very much connected to the living area.

"The kids were more than content to play in the pool for hours. They had as much fun as we did during the week, and they really got to know each other that way—while having a fun

---

* Disney's cruise-ship line offers a seven-night package with this type of room arrangement. On-board entertainment includes kid-friendly options at various hours of the day, opening up private time for adults.

In Tortola, British Virgin Islands, the Long Bay Beach Resort offers a popular "Second Honeymoon" package. Holiday Inn's Sunspree Resort in Jamaica goes further; it can provide a wedding service. Their wedding service includes allowing children to exchange jewelry, just as the adults do.

Popular choices of all-suite hotels include Residence Inn by Marriott and Homewood Suites from Hilton.

vacation," Madelyn recounts. "Because they're so young, we weren't comfortable with sending them down to the pool unsupervised, but we discovered the two of us could have great chats while lounging by the pool. And we took turns going for long walks or browsing in the gift shop while the kids splashed away their cares."

The couple included Sea World in their adventure, solely for the benefit of the children. It's a choice neither of them regrets. "This marriage is not just about us as a couple. It's also about us as a brand-new family unit," Ken explains. "We wanted everyone to feel included, and we wanted our new family to begin in a hugely fun, highly memorable way. We did manage to schedule it during an off-season time, so our hotel bills weren't as horrible as you might think. Madelyn found us discount passes to Sea World, and we discovered that after the big breakfast furnished by the hotel, we could get along for most of the day with just snacks.

"When you add it all up, it just wasn't that expensive," he concludes. "But I'm serious about this: The trip would have been worth it at any price. California was the place where our new family really formed itself."

GOOD REASONS FOR MAKING THE FAMILYMOON a key part of the remarriage might include

- blending two different sets of children into a new household
- sending a message to the children that they are loved and cared about
- simply building some highly positive memories into the lives of the kids to replace some of the pain and difficult memories from divorce or single-parenting

Weighing against the familymoon concept might be the sheer cost of traveling together as a group, especially if airfare is involved. Although most families see quality bonding time as important, most are also limited in the amount of financial resources they can devote to a vacation or familymoon. To many remarriage families, the idea of heading off to a warm state or a tropical paradise is completely out of the question. Attempting to do so would only add to what may already be a high load of debt.

But for those who strongly believe in the idea, it needn't be expensive. Rodger and Julia were blending five children into a new family: her three, his two. Money was extremely limited, yet Rodger was a strong advocate of doing something like a familymoon. Julia quickly agreed to the idea, but she was also worried about the cost.

Their solution? Rodger borrowed a friend's large RV unit. After the wedding, the new family drove just a few hundred miles to a scenic state park, where they parked, cooked food on an outdoor fire for some of their meals, and spent four days and three nights in the beauty of a wooded lakefront area.

"It's true that we didn't have a lot of privacy as a couple," Julia admits. "But we told ourselves we'd make time for privacy later. We told stories at night while everyone was lying in bed trying to sleep. The kids told jokes to each other, and we adults sometimes chimed in. By the end of those four days, we really felt like a family—and we hadn't spent much money at all. We actually did the trip for less than we had budgeted.

"Our biggest expense, as you might imagine, was for groceries. We kind of went overboard on meat, colas for the kids, and desserts like s'mores that we made over a roaring fire. But still, it would have cost us money to feed everyone at home, so the trip itself wasn't that expensive."

Rodger agrees. "Everything worked out well for all of us, and our family started to come together as we camped. My two kids had the best vacation of their lives—and my three new kids seemed to have a lot of fun too."

OTHER REMARRIAGE FAMILIES ON A BUDGET have managed to combine the idea of a family bonding time with a conventional honeymoon. This takes effort in the planning stages, but can be a great success.

"We knew people would be giving us money for our wedding," says the husband of a couple remarried in St. Paul, Minnesota. "So we decided in advance that we'd spend some of that gift money on the children.

"We got married in the morning, had a meal and reception time with all our friends and family, then we took our new family group over to the Mall of America for the rest of the day. We gave each of the kids an equal dollar amount and then we took turns spending the money however the kids chose. Instead of splitting up and going separate ways, we went to the stores as a group, even if only one of us was shopping there.

"It was really informative to see how each child approached the spending of the money they were given," the husband continues. "For example, my new son (the wife's birth child) ran us all over the mall looking for just the right baseball cap he wanted. When he found it, he bought two of them: one for him, one for me. It absolutely blew me away. He had a limited budget to work with, and he spent a lot of his gift money to buy me that hat. Do you have any idea how loved I feel every time I put that hat on?" he says with emotion in his voice.

In addition to the gift monies to be spent by each child, the couple also budgeted for some amusement rides in the mall and planned for a meal time in the food court. And with the long and busy wedding-and-mall day concluded, grandparents took custody of the children for the balance of the weekend. The two adults went off for a quick two-night, one-day honeymoon at a cabin in Wisconsin.

"We had a great time together as a new family," the husband says, "and then my new wife and I got away all by ourselves. I don't know if that would work for all remarriage families or not, but it was the perfect solution for us. By the time we left the kids at the end of our wedding day, they were overfed, well-gifted, and worn out.

"We probably could have used a little more time away from them," he adds with a smile, "because we were worn out by then too. But it was nice to have some peace and quiet in our little cabin, just the two of us."

Kicking Things Off Right

Whether or not your wedding is a major production, and whether or not your newly blending family opts for a honeymoon or a familymoon, the key concept is to be strategic and intentional as you start the new family unit. Being proactive in planning can help things go more smoothly in the early stages of your new life.

The decisions you make will be sending signals to everyone: extended family members, friends, co-workers, and your immediate family circle. Try to be deliberate and focused; talk together as a couple about the goals you're hoping to achieve. Is your new identity as a couple your most important priority? Plan the type of wedding, honeymoon, or both that helps that happen. Is the blending of two sets of children into one new family your highest value? Think carefully, budget with wisdom, and consider a familymoon experience.

Starting out wisely and well can give you a positive "bounce" going into the unavoidable challenges ahead. Making a conscious effort to be united as a couple and as a family can pay great dividends later, when tough choices have to be made about lifestyle, who should discipline the children, and the many other issues you'll have to face—including the one we'll look at in the next chapter: the question of housing.

CHAPTER SEVEN

Your Place or Mine?

Strategies for Choosing Where to Live

❉

Every room of this house has memories for us;
many of them laced with anger and tears.
If we're going to start over—and we need to—then
we really need to find a new place to live.

FAY,
divorced mother of three,
engaged to be married

*Y*OUR PLACE OR MINE?

It's one of the first questions faced by couples choosing to remarry. Whether recovering from the death of a spouse or the pain of a messy divorce, persons who choose to remarry have often lived "alone" for a while. Often they have served as the sole adults and primary caregivers within their households.

Available options may seem equally attractive or equally dismal. He may be living in an apartment while paying substantial alimony to an ex-wife who received their former house in the divorce settlement. She may be recently established in the first "home of her own" while already putting roots down in a location of her choosing.

Both may be renters; or each may own a home. Both may be excited about a change in location; or neither may wish to relocate. As the new relationship gets underway, issues of where to live after marriage immediately rise to the surface, challenging the conflict-resolution skills of the partners.

Discussions may become emotional for one or both persons. The core values and key assumptions of each spouse may differ significantly. Choosing a place to live may involve respecting vastly different value systems.

Deciding where to live can be one of the earliest tests of the problem-solving and conflict-resolution skills of a couple planning to join in marriage. In this chapter, we'll raise some of the issues involved and consider some of the strategic implications of the possible choices. There are many factors to consider in choosing a place to establish your home; there may be a few advisors you'll wish to consult. And you'll receive unsolicited advice as well.

The Totally Empty Nest

Although they may choose to bear or adopt children later, remarried couples establishing a home without children generally face fewer obstacles while setting up a household.

Even so, the decision about where to live may not be a simple one.

Ron and Barb were each the parents of older children. Her children were college age and above, and were living in other cities, thus they were not a factor in any housing decision. His kids were in the custody of their birth mother. On the surface, it appeared they would be setting up a household in which children were not an issue, yet this was not the case. Being close to his children was an extremely high priority for Ron.

"I told Barbara as we talked about getting married that I'd live in any kind of housing, grand or simple, but it had to be a five-minute drive from my kids," Ron explains. "They're in middle school and high school now. Regardless of how things worked out with their mom and me, I'm not going to be an absentee father. I'm always going to be there for them!"

This was a key issue that Ron brought to the table as he and

Barbara decided where to live. At the time, he was living in an apartment; Barb owned a house about a half-hour away.

"I wasn't excited about giving up my house, especially at first," she admits. "But the more Ron talked about his kids it was obvious that this was a high priority for him. As we talked about it, instead of resenting him over this whole issue, I became really proud of him. He's a great dad to those kids!"

Their eventual decision? Purchasing a new condominium unit as a couple. The condo was within the radius specified by Ron; for Barbara, the main attraction was that it was brand-new.

"We got to choose our colors, our flooring, our lighting, and everything!" she enthuses. "It was the first time I'd ever been able to plan my own kitchen, my own bathrooms, my own home. So it really helped soften the blow of selling the house I was living in. My house, although I loved it, was an older home already needing frequent repairs.

"We moved into a brand-new condo, finished exactly as we had chosen, and now I'm spoiled by the exercise room, the pool complex, and the sauna. And to think, I didn't want to leave my aging, paint-peeling house!"

She laughs at the recollection, although the process was sometimes uncomfortable. Happily, the couple found a workable solution together.

THE CHOICES ARE SIMPLER—but may still involve substantial negotiation—when children are not a factor in any way. Neither Larry nor Janet had any children when they got married—Larry for the second time, Janet for her first. Both were homeowners; both wanted to keep their homes. The discussion of where to live became lively, and at times frustrating.

"Both of us probably should have been 'let's have it your way' or something like that," Janet laments. "But both of us were very stubborn about it. We each wanted to stay in our own home and have the other person move in."

The couple made progress on every other issue. They came

to agreement on virtually all of the major choices they were con-
fronting—except for the thorny question of where to live. Faced
with repeated failures to reach a compromise in this matter, they
eventually consulted friends.

"My friend Becky was like, 'Sell both houses, buy something
new!' and that's what we eventually did," Janet reveals. "I don't
know why that hadn't occurred to us; maybe because we were
too busy fighting about it."

Any regrets now, after the fact?

"Yeah, I regret being so stubborn," Larry sighs. "Our new
place is much better than what either one of us was living in
before. And I probably should have just agreed to move in with
Janet instead of being so pigheaded."

"We were both pigheaded," Janet chimes in.

A Fresh Start

Without children to consider, the issues involved in choosing
housing may center on ownership versus renting, commuting
time and proximity to employers, or perhaps a desire to be
located near a church or in a specific section of the city. Also a
factor: Many couples simply prefer to begin a new relationship
by making a fresh start in housing that is new to both.

As we'll discover, the issue of housing-related memories may
come into play. If either partner is living in a home once shared
with a former spouse, the new adult may not feel comfortable
moving into it.

This opinion appears equally shared among genders. "Gail
was living in the same house where she and her husband had
raised their kids," relates Dan. "The kids were grown and gone,
but the memories were still there. It felt weird to consider
moving into the same bedroom where Gail had lived with her
previous husband. I felt very uncomfortable about that."

Sharon's perspective is very similar. "Mike and his ex had
lived together in the same place where Mike was living as we
started dating. He was totally fine with me moving in and us

two living there together, but it didn't feel right to me. I don't know why, really; it just seemed like I was invading someone else's space. Or maybe it felt like I would be competing with memories of someone else if I lived in that same exact house."

Different housing may be a wise option to consider if at all possible. Beginning a new relationship within a new space is a fresh start for everyone. If it's simply not an option to consider purchasing or renting a different place, it may be wise to allow the incoming partner to suggest major changes in the décor, arrangement, or furnishings. This helps visually reinforce the reality that the old partner is gone and a new household is being established.

As with all issues you discuss with your remarriage partner, be sure to share your feelings openly without holding anything back. In this way, you'll help guarantee that any decision you both make will be inclusive of the true emotions and true values of each person.

One Has Children—the Other Doesn't

If one of you is busy raising children, a number of issues immediately impact your choice of where to live. Children of divorce, no matter how amicably their parents now relate to each other, are likely to be living with more than a few unresolved emotional traumas.

Should children be moved to a new setting as a new family is established, or should children be allowed the continuity of staying in their existing home? This is a key question in the housing issue. There are as many points of view as there are possibilities.

"I didn't want my children to change schools," Nancy tells us. "They had been through so much change already, with their dad leaving us and with all of us having to move from our beautiful home into a crowded apartment. It took a while, especially for my youngest, but all of them finally adjusted to the apartment and things were gradually becoming what, for us, is the 'new normal.'

"When I started seriously dating Clarence, one of the things I told him is that I wasn't going to move my kids. They were staying in the same apartment, and going to the same schools, period. I wouldn't even consider moving them."

Clarence agreed to move into the apartment—as a starting point. It may have helped that Nancy's ex-husband had never lived in this space. It may also have helped that he was already an apartment dweller.

Did staying in the same apartment seem to help the children adjust?

"I think so," Nancy volunteers. "Clarence had already been spending a lot of time in the apartment while we were dating. The kids were used to him being around us a lot of the time. It wasn't such a major change for them when we got married and he moved in. Nobody had to give up their room or go through a whole bunch of new changes."

Do they plan to stay in this apartment for the future?

"I hope not," Clarence opines. "I really want us to buy a house. I agree about keeping the kids in their same schools, but I'd like for us to buy a house instead of wasting all our money on rent every month!"

Nancy is silent for a moment. "I think the kids need a little more time," she suggests. "But in the future it might be nice to find a house in this same neighborhood, if we can afford it. I'm not open at all to moving the kids to a new school district or a different area. They've had enough hassles already, with their dad and me splitting up."

Changing Schools—Always a Negative?

"My daughter was having a horrible experience in middle school," Jordan begins. "I was the custodial parent. I knew she was having a really bad time, mostly with some peer problems, but I didn't know how to really help her. She went through about six months of depression, not wanting to go to school, withdrawing herself from almost everything. And at about the same time, I was getting serious in my relationship with Janelle."

As the relationship between Jordan and Janelle progressed, and as marriage became a serious consideration, Jordan felt divinely inspired one day to have his potential wife do some "counseling" with his teenage daughter.

"I was praying for Mindy one morning. I just felt like I should ask Janelle to take Mindy out for coffee to see if she could find out what the problems were at school. Janelle liked the idea, but neither of us knew if it would work. Mindy hadn't been talking to either of us, except in one-word answers, for a long time."

Sometimes, miracles do happen. Over iced coffee at Starbucks, Mindy was at first reserved and withdrawn. Janelle kept silent, waiting patiently as Mindy became more comfortable with the conversation. What she discovered was that Mindy was pressured and persecuted by her peers at school. An hour became three hours; the coffee time extended into the early evening. As one cup led to another, Mindy poured out a torrent of emotions and feelings, clearly exhausted by the effort of holding things within herself for so long.

Later in the conversation, when Janelle asked Mindy if she saw any possible solutions to the problems she faced, her answer was immediate.

"I want to go to Horizon [Christian School]," she responded quickly. "I think I need to start all over again, with new friends."

Jordan was astounded to learn of his daughter's desire to change schools. "She had never mentioned that, not even once!" he remembers. "I had tried to talk to her several times, but she would never explain what was really going on."

The couple talked at length about the issue, both with and without Mindy's input. Eventually, as the couple planned their wedding, they decided that paying for Mindy's tuition at Horizon would be a major priority for them, even though their financial resources would be stretched to the limit.

"It did affect our choice about where to live," Janelle recounts. "With paying for Mindy's tuition as a high priority, we realized we probably couldn't buy the house we had been looking at. Instead, we started house-shopping in an area closer to Mindy's new school, in a neighborhood with lower-priced homes."

Mindy was more than ready to move from her old home. "I really hate it here," she admitted when asked about going or staying. "I don't have any friends here. I just want to start over."

And three years after their wedding, more than two years after enrolling Mindy in a private high school, Jordan and Janelle have no regrets about their choices.

IT'S NATURAL AND USEFUL for the children's well-being to be a major consideration in choosing where to live. This does not mean that the children themselves should make the decision; rather, both adults should carefully weigh the strategic reasons for keeping the children where they are—or for giving them a fresh start in a new location.

In general, younger children are more flexible and adapt more easily to changes in their social environment. Children of preschool age may be excited about a move, not really grasping its full meaning. Teens, however, can usually be expected to have a negative opinion about moving. Their priorities tend to revolve around friendship with peers, and thoughts of moving can be scary.

Expect children to be ambivalent about making changes in their lives, especially about making a major change such as housing, school, or city. Let each child voice his or her true feelings, pay attention to each perspective, then make a decision that reflects and values the input received.

In the short term, ignoring a child's voice or overriding a child's opinion may seem easier. In the longer term, however, many future heartaches can be avoided by listening wisely, planning carefully, and including everyone in the process of establishing a new home.

When Both of You Have Children at Home

Welcome to the most challenging of all scenarios.

You have children living at home; your spouse does also. Now you've decided to get married. As you'll soon discover, the decision to marry is the last "simple" decision you'll make. From here on out, life gets difficult quickly.

Where do you live when two sets of children have their own home? Or, as remarriage families often frame the question, who wins?

Your mission, if you choose to accept it, is to create a housing strategy which lets everyone win, or which lets no one win. By sharing the victory, sharing the pain, or both, you give your new family unit the best odds of making it work.

JAMES AND JULIE DIDN'T REALIZE how much was at stake. James was the custodial father of two daughters, ages 11 and 13. Julie was the parent of two—a son, 12, and a daughter, almost 10.

Julie was living in a two-story house that she and her ex-husband had built to their specifications in a wonderful neighborhood. The home had four bedrooms and two large living areas. There was more than enough space for James and his two daughters to join them.

They were living in what James termed "the alimony apartment," a two-bedroom unit with less than a thousand square feet of living space. Although he enjoyed the simplicity of apartment living, the chance to live in a nice house again was too much for him to pass up. Without consulting the kids, the couple made a decision they would live in Julie's home after the wedding.

To James, it seemed like a no-brainer. "My daughters were sharing a tiny bedroom in my apartment," James remembers. "The apartment had only one bathroom. They'd be sharing a bedroom in Julie's house also, but it would be a much larger room, with its own bathroom attached. They'd have more room, more privacy, more of everything!"

Julie recalls being equally excited about the housing choice. "I didn't want my kids to have to move," she sighs. "And there was no way that all six of us would fit into James's apartment. It seemed easy: We'd all live in the big house where my kids and I were already living."

Looking back, the first complication seems easy enough to predict. Julie's daughter had been living in the largest bedroom of the house, the one with a walk-in closet and an attached bathroom. Since there would be two girls, James' daughters, sharing a bedroom, it made sense to move them into the larger bedroom, displacing Julie's daughter into a smaller bedroom nearby.

The fireworks began almost immediately. Julie's daughter, upset about losing "her room" to the new siblings, refused to cooperate about anything. She was implacable: yelling at her mother, stalking off to her room instead of eating her dinner, acting out in every possible way.

James's two daughters, who at first had loved their new room, quickly got tired of hearing their new sister insist it was "her room," as she continued to call it. They would come home from school and find treasured items of clothing, or personal items of jewelry, missing from their closets and dresser drawers.

The three girls fought constantly, with the parents trying desperately not to take sides or show favoritism. The result was a daily round of arguing, fighting, and discussing, then repeating the same cycle the next day. Nothing worked.

In order to win, the adults decided they'd first have to lose. Living in the home's master bedroom, they decided to vacate that space and let James's daughters have it instead. That would mean that Julie's daughter could have her room back. It would also mean that the newlyweds would live in a small bedroom without its own bathroom attached.

The strategy worked—sort of. The girls quit fighting after the room swap was completed; however, they rarely related to each other, preferring not to speak to one another at all. The new room arrangement resulted in the cessation of outright war, but it did nothing at all to contribute to a meaningful and lasting peace.

Two years into their marriage, James and Julie are seeing some positive signs that the girls are getting along better, but as James admits, "It's been a very slow process. We're not sure the girls will ever really be friends, but at least they don't fight any more, and sometimes they even share clothes voluntarily."

"My daughter was definitely the 'princess' type," Julie confesses. "And I hadn't realized how impossible it would be to have three candidates all vying for the title of 'princess' in our new family."

James and Julie's experience highlights some of the difficulties involved when one family keeps its home and another family moves in alongside it. Even with careful planning, the possibilities for perceived injustice are limitless.

TINA AND BILL HAD A SIMPLER TASK. Each brought only one child to the new family unit. Bill's ex-wife had fled the state, and Tina's ex-husband was incarcerated. Bill was living with his young son in a trailer; Tina shared a bedroom with her young daughter in Tina's parents' home.

The newlyweds moved into Bill's trailer—and the arrangement worked.

"I prefer to call it a modular home," Bill says of his doublewide trailer. "It's in a nice park with a small pool. We have great neighbors. Everyone really looks out for each other. There are a lot of retired couples in here."

The three-bedroom home had one empty bedroom when Tina and her daughter moved in. With Bill and Tina sharing the master bedroom, Bill's son and Tina's daughter—both under age six—could have their own rooms.

"Our kids got along great, just like we did," Tina beams. "One of the first things we noticed was how well our two kids played together. Bill's son is a little bit older (two years) than my daughter, and the two of them are best buds. Casey was so happy to get her own room, and I was so glad to move out of my folks' house, that both of us were delighted to move in with Bill. We didn't really worry about the kids getting along."

Bill and Tina's experience may not be typical. Their situation was greatly aided by the presence of only one child in each household, by the difference in genders of the two children, and by the closeness in the ages of the two. Clearly, the move represented a "win–win" situation—Tina and her daughter moved into a better arrangement, while Bill and his son stayed in their comfortable home and gained new roommates.

As we've seen, remarriage families frequently experience trauma and difficulty when trying to blend two family units into space previously occupied by just one. While the adults may have little trouble adjusting, the children may take months to settle into new routines. As they do, their responses may be negative instead of positive, confounding the expectations of adults who had hoped everything would go well.

It's often difficult for a remarried couple to look at the housing issue from the perspective of the children. Typically, they make decisions about where to live based primarily on financial factors. Also typically, they tend to have an overoptimistic view of how the kids will respond.

Is it completely impossible to blend two families into the home that one occupied previously? Perhaps not, but it's nearly so. If the children are not fully involved in the discussion from the start, there may be very little hope of having a successful and positive transition. The older the children, the more critical it is to involve their perspective in any serious discussion about where to live.

New for Everyone

Space that is new for everyone is often the least difficult choice. As we noted earlier, this can be viewed as "lose-lose" since everyone is giving up their previous home. Yet if managed wisely and well, it can emerge as a "win-win" since everyone is gaining a fresh start in a new environment. Plan for an experience in which "everyone gives, everyone gains" as you decide where to live.

Henry and Raquel did so, and have few regrets. "I guess we'd be a 'lose–lose' from most perspectives," Henry notes. "Both of us had school-age children, and we lived in separate school districts and areas. If we had moved our new family into either one of our two homes, one set of kids would have given up their schools while the other set kept everything the same.

"We aren't the brightest of people, but we could see that wouldn't work. How could we possibly decide whose kids had to lose, and whose kids could win? We never seriously considered living in either of our two houses."

Not that everything went smoothly—quite the contrary.

"My house sold in a hurry," Raquel says with a smile. "Henry's house didn't seem like it would ever sell. We closed on the new house after my house sold, but then we were making two house payments. We couldn't afford that, and it went on for nearly six months. We were going crazy!"

"The good news is, it was a complete change for everybody," Henry says. "The bad news is, it was a complete change for everybody. All of us were mourning the loss of our former homes—all of us were enjoying the new house.

"Besides all that, the financial stress of trying to pay for two houses, which we couldn't afford, was really keeping me awake at night. We finally sold my house—probably for less than we should have, but we needed to get out from under it. The day we finally closed on it, we had a family party!"

He shrugs his shoulders. "We needed that party; it was time for a celebration after all our struggles."

Not everything was difficult. Some typical hassles were unusually smooth for the new family.

Raquel's daughter, the oldest among the two sets of children, was just finishing middle school as the couple got married and moved.

"She would have been changing schools anyway," Raquel recalls. "And just as we were planning our move, her best friend moved to Boston. So in a lot of ways, I think God helped our family have an easier move than we might have had otherwise. My daughter didn't want to move at first, but when she saw the new house, and when we toured the high school she'd be attending, she started to change her opinion about everything."

Four years after remarrying, Henry and Raquel have no regrets about the housing decision they made when getting married. "This place is 'home' for our family," Henry says, as Raquel nods agreement. "This is where we became a family. This is where we started our new life together. Like the book says, there's a lot of laughter in these walls."

CHAPTER EIGHT

Who's the Boss?

Strategies for Healthy and Constructive Discipline

✼

Discipline your children
while they are young enough to learn.
If you don't, you are
helping them destroy themselves.

PROVERBS 19:18

ONE OF THE EARLY TESTS of an original marriage is the discipline of children. A husband and wife may come together in a loving and positive union, yet when they begin to raise a family, they discover they have different approaches to the teaching and training of their children.

In a remarriage, this test may come even earlier, since one or both of the partners may already be involved in raising children. Particularly when one has experience as a parent and the other does not, there may be heated arguments about whether the children are being properly trained.

The person who has never tried to raise a child is usually the expert. He or she may have wonderful theories, some of them derived from college courses in psychology or sociology, about the way in which a child should be encouraged.

Meanwhile, the birth parent, who has already lived through the failure of most of her theories, has discovered by experience

123

what actually works. She may be fiercely protective of her children, and protective also of the way in which she as a mother handles matters of discipline, teaching, and consequences.

He as a father may be very permissive with his children, afraid to be firm with them lest he lose their affection. Having experienced the loss of his marriage partner, he is emotionally afraid of losing his children as well. To keep them loyal and supportive, he may indulge his children by giving them whatever they want, whenever they want it—in effect avoiding his valid role of parental authority.

Remarried couples do a lot of arguing in their first few years as a couple. If one or both has brought children into the new union, many of the arguments will revolve around the way in which the children are being raised.

Is there a right way, a best way, or at least a very wise way to raise children in the context of a remarriage partnership? In this chapter, we'll look at some strategies remarried couples are finding effective. Consider these as starting points rather than comprehensive manuals on parenting. If you're already involved in the training of a child, you're already becoming an expert on your own challenges.

Trust the wisdom that is emerging within you, particularly as you pray for guidance in the raising of your children. Along with that wisdom, consider the following ideas that other remarried couples have discovered by experience as they teach, train, pray for, and try to raise their families effectively.

Let the Birth Parent Be the Boss Parent

"You're not my mommy!"

Jennifer was growing tired of hearing that phrase as she struggled to discipline her new husband's four-year-old daughter. Every time Jennifer attempted to establish some authority with the child, her response was immediate, rebellious, and loud.

"I don't have to do what you say!" the little girl would assert loudly. "You're not my real mommy!"

Jennifer knew her husband was not the source of this idea in his little girl. Was her husband's ex-wife, the birth mother of this child, planting the seeds of this rebellious attitude? Or was this act of defiance a normal part of the child's growth and development process?

Three months into an otherwise successful remarriage, Jennifer didn't care where the problem had come from—she just wanted a solution! Meanwhile her new husband was checking out of the parental role, glad that his daughter finally had a mother in the house again. Jennifer's growing frustration—and her husband's continuing avoidance of the issue—eventually brought the couple to a minister for marriage counseling.

They were almost too late. Jennifer was ready to walk out on the remarriage and not come back. Daily defiance from an angry four-year-old can do that to a person!

The Roles Are Already Filled

Even if a couple has spent a lot of time together before getting remarried, integrating a new adult into the household poses difficulties for any child, and it presents special difficulties for younger children. With the role of "mommy" and "daddy" already filled in a child's universe, it is entirely unclear where and how the new adult fits into the picture. Efforts to explain the idea of "new mommy" or "new daddy" often fail to clarify the matter in the mind of a young child, since "real mommy" or "real daddy" may still live nearby.

Experienced remarriage couples are nearly universal in their belief that phrases like "new mommy" should be avoided with younger children. Instead, it may be simpler to use terms like "Daddy's new friend" or the more accurate phrase "Daddy's new wife." The authority that will eventually flow from this relationship will be based on the new partner's role as an adult, rather than as a perceived parent. Adults can and should have appropriate authority over children regardless of whether or not they are in the role of parents.

As the new family unit is formed, and as issues of authority rise to prominence in the household, the most logical and natural approach is to permit the birth parent to be the boss parent, especially in the early stages of the union. This does not usurp or undermine the authority of the new adult; rather, it allows the child a chance to adjust to the idea that another adult has entered his or her universe. The child should already have, or should quickly gain, a respect for all adults in areas of appropriate authority and training.

Trying to become the "new mommy" is an exercise in futility. The child may naturally prefer its existing mother or father (whichever is absent) to the new partner of the other parent. Although setting up competition among parents is always an unwise idea, it is especially unhelpful as a new union is formed. New adults should make absolutely no effort to displace the role of an existing parent or to assume the role as the new boss in the home.

In Jennifer's case, her new husband needed to be directly involved in the discipline of his little girl. The husband also needed to gradually train his daughter to respect, relate properly to, and obey the new woman in the home.

This was frustrating news to the husband, who admitted getting remarried partly with the purpose of "finding a mother for my little girl." When he said "finding a mother," what he seemed to mean was "getting back to my life, without the stress of coping with my young child's constant need for attention."

This particular man had hoped that getting remarried was his ticket back to the glory days of being childless and free. Although he loved his daughter, he was emotionally exhausted from always trying to cope with her. "You're a woman," he said to his new partner, "so I know you'll know what to do with her."

Not only did Jennifer *not* know what to do, she was tired of trying!

Have you been in Jennifer's situation, or do you know someone who is trying to find a valid authority role in the life of someone else's children?

In the early phases of a remarriage, the birth parent should reign supreme in matters of child discipline and training. The new adult should observe, learn, and reinforce the birth parent's style of parenting, even if the new adult might approach some issues differently.

ALTHOUGH IN JENNIFER'S CASE IT WAS the husband and father who wanted relief from his parental duties, it might just as easily be a mother who is ready to check out and get some much-needed rest. Carol, busy raising two teenaged sons, could hardly wait for Mark to join their household.

"He's a man!" she proclaimed joyously. "My boys will listen to him!"

Carol was frustrated and upset when reality happened. Her sons refused to respect Mark's advice and counsel. They directly disobeyed him when he tried to issue a command or bark out an order. Carol didn't understand why this was happening. She was confused and discouraged.

"Ever since they became teens, they haven't listened to me," she complained to her counselor. "I know all they need is a man in the house, someone they can look up to and respect."

Yet Carol's sons defied Mark and refused to accept his instruction.

"What am I doing wrong?" Mark asked the counselor. "I've tried to reason with them, I've tried explaining myself, and I've tried just giving orders. Nothing works! Where am I failing? What can I do differently?"

The answer was not particularly comforting. "Carol, it's still your turn to be the parent," the counselor insisted. "This is your home, these are your sons, and the bottom line is—it is your responsibility to teach them to respect you as a person and to respect your authority. Having a man in the house changes nothing at all about your role as a mother and an adult."

This was not at all what Carol wanted to hear. In many ways, it is easier to find a new partner than it is to learn how to cope with rebellious adolescent males, especially when they're larger, taller, and stronger than their overworked mother. Carol didn't want to learn how to get control—she wanted her new husband to take charge, boss the boys into obedience, and run the family!

It was exactly the same with Jennifer's husband: He could hardly wait until a new mother came on the scene so that *she* could do all the hard work of raising his young daughter. When the daughter didn't cooperate, and when Jennifer didn't seem to know what to do, the husband was intensely frustrated.

Getting remarried is not the solution to the discipline problems you encounter as a parent. Establishing yourself as the authority in the lives of your children is your own role, not someone else's. No matter how difficult it seems, your task is to be the parent. Get the help you need from a school counselor, from supportive friends, from your priest, rabbi, or minister, or from a paid professional counselor. The life skills you'll gain will benefit you personally, will improve the lives and behavior of your children, and will greatly improve the chances of your remarriage being a successful and lasting union.

A Second Adult Can Be Helpful

While the birth parent sets the boundaries, enforces the rules, and decides on appropriate consequences for disobedience, there is definite value to the addition of a second adult in the household. A second adult can provide an extension of the parent's authority and give support to the parent who performs the primary role.

The task of the second adult in the household, whether male or female, is to support and reinforce the authority of the birth parent. When managed well, the role of the second adult can indeed provide immense relief to the weary and overstressed birth parent who is worn out from coping with rebellion. Yet the form of this relief will not be to "take over" the duties; rather, it will be to agree with and reinforce the boundaries as an encouragement to the one who is in charge.

One way of looking at the role of this second adult is to consider this person much like a grandparent or other trusted relative. When grandparents function effectively, they do not undermine or usurp the parent's role. Rather, they reinforce it by echoing the same rules, establishing the same boundaries, and providing the same consequences—or reporting disobedience to the parent, who then provides the appropriate consequences.

Imagine how destructive it might be if grandparents did not reinforce the boundaries of the parent in raising the children.

Suppose a young single mother leaves her two children in the care of their grandparents for a day, or perhaps even for a week. No sooner has the mother left for work than the grandparents quickly begin changing all the rules.

"I know your mommy doesn't let you have cookies," the grandmother might say, "but I've just baked a huge batch of chocolate-chip cookies and they're fresh out of the oven. Why don't you run into the kitchen and help yourself? Just eat all you want—they won't hurt you!"

Or suppose the grandfather says, "I know your mom makes you go to bed by eight o'clock every night, but I think that's way too early. Here's the remote control for the television—stay up as late as you want! Just be sure to turn off the TV before you go to bed, okay?"

Would you want to be the mother of these children after they'd spent a week with grandparents like these? After all your hard work of trying to set rules and establish good boundaries for your children, you'd find your efforts undermined.

Bring in the Reinforcements

But consider a much different way in which the scenario might unfold.

When leaving your children with their grandparents, you

explain that bedtime is eight o'clock, without exceptions. You explain your "no cookies" rule, or whatever boundary you have established in your own home.

The minute you're gone, the kids begin testing the limits.

"We want to watch David Letterman tonight!" they all scream in chorus. But Grandpa is wise to their tricks, and simply smiles.

"Okay," he says, "I'll record the show, and we can watch it together tomorrow during the daytime. Your bedtime is eight o'clock tonight, remember?"

Or perhaps the kids run into the kitchen. "Grandma," they suggest innocently, "can you show us how to bake chocolate-chip cookies? We want to learn how to cook just like you do. You're such a great chef!"

And Grandma smiles at their flattery but sees right through it.

"How wonderful!" she exclaims. "I'm just about to bake some low-fat oat-bran muffins. That will be perfect since your mom has a 'no cookies' rule. She's such a smart lady—she knows exactly what's best for you!"

Imagine getting your children back from a week in that environment. Instead of being undermined and disrespected, your role as a parent has been reinforced and supported all week long by these other adults. Their support and agreement has made your role as a parent a lot easier. They have united themselves behind your appropriate authority and have enforced the same boundaries with your children, on your behalf and at your request. They have become a valued part of your parenting team—not by replacing you but by reinforcing your role as a wise, caring parent who has set limits in good and appropriate places.

A second adult who functions in this way can dramatically improve the morale of an overworked single parent, consistently increasing the odds that the children will obey the rules, stay within the limits, and learn to behave wisely. This type of second adult in the home can be God's good gift to the household.

To draw on a further illustration, when police officers have a partner assigned to them, one of the primary tasks of the partner is to "watch the back" of the other officer. In other words, the partner has a protective role, defending the officer in cases where danger may be coming from many different directions. In the line of duty, an officer needs to know someone is watching his or her back so he or she is protected.

In much the same way, a second adult in the household should "watch the back" of the birth parent, protecting respect for that parent and thus defending the rules, values, boundaries, and consequences he or she has established. When the role is understood in this way, the birth parent quickly gains confidence in the second adult, establishing a relationship of mutual trust.

An equally important development is that the children of the household learn to show more respect for their natural parent. The daily presence of a second adult who is busy reinforcing the wisdom, virtue, and parameters established by the birth parent helps children learn valid and appropriate respect for authority. Although they can be counted on to test the limits, kids will do better once they realize the limits are being supported, affirmed, and reinforced by the new adult in the home.

Don't Try to Be Liked—Try to Be Fair

Let's face it; it's tough to be the new adult in a remarriage household. You're busy trying to establish a husband-and-wife relationship and show your love for your new partner. In the midst of that, you're getting better acquainted with your partner's children, hoping they'll accept you in this unfamiliar role.

Wanting to be liked by your spouse's children is normal and natural. However, it also has the potential to undermine your eventual emergence as a respected adult in the new family unit. You'll need to realize your own desire to be liked. You'll also want to keep that desire firmly in check. Instead of trying to be *liked* by the children, work on trying to be *fair*.

WHEN JARED MARRIED CINDY, her three younger children had been told that homework came first, before play, as they returned from school in the afternoon. In the early days of the remarriage, Jared was home when the kids returned from school but Cindy was still at work.

"I didn't agree with her rules at all," Jared recalls. "Those poor kids had been at school all day already, and she wanted them to come home and start doing homework before they had any fun. I thought that was horrible!"

He quickly became popular with the kids by ignoring his wife's rules. When they returned home from school each day, he would play outdoors with them instead of insisting that their homework be done.

Jared achieved his goal of being liked by the children. They loved him, and why wouldn't they? It was a lot more fun playing outdoors all afternoon with a new adult friend than it was to go inside, sit down, and work through the piles of homework assigned by their teachers.

Jared became the kids' new best friend. But you can guess how things went in his marriage relationship.

"I couldn't believe it!" Cindy says passionately. "I had worked so hard to establish rules for my kids, and here he was completely ignoring everything I'd set up!"

The discipline of the children, or rather the lack of that discipline—as Cindy saw the issue—quickly led the couple to arguing, fighting, and stress. They turned to a counselor for help and advice. In this case, Cindy's point of view was the one most affirmed.

"The counselor said I had to start enforcing Cindy's rules." Jared grimaces as he recalls the outcome. "She insisted that Cindy's rules had to be respected by everyone in the household, including me. So I did what the counselor said, but then the kids hated me! I went from being their friend to being their enemy, all at once. I really thought I'd lost them."

For a while, Jared did lose the affection of the children.

Meanwhile, he was gaining their respect in ways he did not fully realize. Here is how Cassandra, age ten, explains the history of the family.

"At first, Jared was a lot of fun," she says. "He was almost like a big brother to us, playing with us every day. Then after that, he got mean and was just exactly like Mom all the time. It was awful, but I guess we needed it. I mean, we already knew what Mom's rules were, so we already knew we were wrong. What would happen to us if we kept getting away with everything?"

Cassandra is wise beyond her years. Even as a child, she realizes that when children learn to disobey and disrespect adults rather than properly following their valid authority, no one wins. What happens to children who keep "getting away with everything"? Their process of maturity is delayed or perhaps permanently impaired. They may move on to chronological adulthood, but they may not progress to a mature and full understanding of how to function in adult society.

When Jared began to act in the way prescribed by the counselor, he lost the friendship and affection of the children—for a while. Gradually, he made a gain that was even more important. He gained their respect, while increasing their respect for their mother and thus for the boundaries she had established. He progressed from "friend" to "foe" to "fair" in their eyes.

Today, although stress points remain in the relationship, Jared and Cindy are in agreement about how to set boundaries for the children.

Two Sets of Children—Two Approaches to Discipline

Karen and Paul had decided to remarry. Each was the custodial parent of several children. As they began to get to know each other's children, they realized that their approaches to issues of discipline were very different. Finding agreement in this became a primary task for them, yet they seemed to make little progress. Karen thought Paul was being entirely too lenient with his children; Paul believed Karen was overcompensating for the lack of a father by being too tough with her kids.

Both of them believed that unless they agreed in advance about how to discipline all of the children—in the same way— the marriage relationship would probably never work. They believed themselves ready to remarry in every other area, yet the issue of appropriate discipline became increasingly difficult for them. Eventually they turned to a professional counselor for advice on the topic.

The counselor's opinion was surprising to both. "Basically, she told us we should each keep disciplining our own children the same way we always had," Paul remembers. "Meanwhile, each of us should support and affirm the other partner's rules with their own children. So she was telling us to have two styles of discipline in our house, rather than one."

Karen was equally perplexed. "We thought the kids needed to be treated fairly," she shares. "And we both thought that treating the kids fairly meant treating them all the same way, not having two different standards of discipline in the house."

The counselor clearly disagreed. "The children are adjusting to enough changes already," she insisted, "without each of you trying to modify or change the rules of your own homes at the same time. Each of you should keep the rules you already have for your own children, rather than trying to mix everybody into a brand-new system."

Karen and Paul both disagreed at first. However, as they talked further, away from the counselor's office, they realized they didn't have a better idea to suggest. They had no solutions of their own to offer.

"We disagreed with each other's approaches, and we also disagreed with the counselor's advice!" Paul laughs. "We were good at disagreeing."

EVENTUALLY, TAKING THE COUNSELOR'S ADVICE seemed like the best of the possible compromises. Karen sat down with her children and explained that her rules were going to continue, although Paul might have different rules for his own children. Paul sat down with his kids and had a similar discussion. All of this occurred while Karen and Paul were dating seriously, but before they combined their two households into one new family.

"I expected my kids to say, 'Hey, that's unfair,' or something," Karen says. "I thought once they saw how lenient Paul was, they'd be jealous of his kids."

Paul grins. "And I thought my kids would realize I was Superdad. I just knew that once they saw how tough Karen was with her kids, they'd be totally grateful for my wisdom in being more relaxed with them…"

The actual response of the children surprised the new couple.

"My daughter said something like 'I'm glad Karen doesn't boss me around like that' and I started to smile," Paul recalls. "Then she said, 'But wow, they sure are well-behaved kids, aren't they?' and I almost fell out of my chair.

"As the oldest of all our combined children, she had already figured out that Karen was doing a good job as a parent, even before I managed to realize that," he admits.

Karen's children surprised her also.

"My son basically said, 'Hey, Paul's kids totally get away with murder.' And I thought to myself, *Oh no, here it comes*." She smiles. "But then he said something like 'I'm glad you don't let us get away with stuff like that' and I almost laughed out loud. My son was telling me that he actually *liked* the way I was doing the discipline in my house. I couldn't believe what I was hearing!"

The pair shares a lengthy chuckle, then both begin praising the advice they received.

"The counselor was absolutely right," Paul insists, looking back. "What we needed was to keep treating our kids the same way we always had. I don't know why we couldn't see that—we were too busy trying to agree with each other, when we really didn't."

Karen concurs. "We only went to a counselor as a last resort. We thought we couldn't afford a counselor, and we hoped we didn't need one. But that was some of the best money we spent as we were first getting together. The wisdom of that counselor helped us know how to manage our kids in those early days."

So, do the two remarriage partners completely agree on approaches to discipline these days? Are all of the kids being treated exactly the same way?

"I don't know," Karen laughs. "I do think Paul has softened me up as we've worked through all this. I think I've been able to relax in some ways and not take every single thing so seriously."

"And I'm definitely more of a hard case now," Paul remarks, smiling. "I watched Karen have such smooth control of her kids and I decided I really wanted that. But I had to get there gradually. I couldn't just change everything all at once. I think I'm closer to Karen's style with my youngest than with my other two."

Karen and Paul learned from the counselor, learned from their children, then learned from each other. Over time, each of their styles changed somewhat. Meanwhile, the kids experienced continuity of discipline as the family bonded.

Finding Agreement on Appropriate Approaches to Discipline

Few topics about parenting are more divisive than the question of how and when to discipline children. Some insist that physical punishment is not only an appropriate way for parents to respond, it is often the most effective way. Others assert that striking or spanking a child is never the best approach, positing that methods such as "time-out" or the withdrawal of favors are to be preferred.

Talking together about the discipline of children is one of the most powerfully effective ways you can prepare for your remarriage relationship. Perhaps only financial matters have the power to be equally destructive within the new relationship you are forming; therefore, you need to take action in advance to consider how you will approach the discipline issue.

Before you remarry, be certain that each partner understands the rules and boundaries the birth parents have established for the children. If these rules and boundaries vary, as is likely, agree together to help enforce each other's views as the new household is being established.

Changing the rules as the new household is forming confuses children and adds uncertainty to the challenges they are already facing. Continuity of discipline and enforcement is in the best interest of the children, and of everyone. Even if the adults disagree profoundly, they should support each other as the new household is bonding and making adjustments.

OVER TIME, THOUGH, IT WILL BE DIFFICULT for a second adult in the household to affirm and help enforce boundaries if he or she is not in general agreement with the theory of discipline already being used by the birth parent. Thus, away from the children, out of the heat of the battle, the adults in the household need to talk frequently and at length about how best to approach issues of child control.

Discussions about rules and boundaries should be held out of earshot of the children, and at times when neither adult is particularly emotional about the topics being considered. Rather than forcing agreement on each other, strive for a genuine understanding of your partner's perspective. Recognize one simple fact: No one understands your partner's children better than your partner does; no one is more qualified to be their parent than your partner is.

If your discussions tend to lead to arguing or fighting, keep things civil. Show respect for your partner and keep your emotions in check. Avoid insults and anger; demonstrate your love by listening more than you speak. It is entirely possible that your views of appropriate discipline will evolve and change over the years, so be open to more education. If each of you has children, be especially open to receiving the lessons each partner has already learned in the parenting process.

All of us are enrolled in the school of parenting. None of us has earned the right to be a tenured professor. Learn from what works; discover how to set aside your ideas when something more effective comes along. Keep learning and growing, and don't expect perfection of yourself, your partner, or your children.

CHAPTER NINE

Blend It Like
the Bradys

Strategies for Forming a "Blended Family"

❋

So-called "blended families"
may not fully blend,
yet they can and do learn to live
together with respect.

IKE AND CAROL BRADY MAKE IT look so easy.

Four females: classic blondes with great hair and smart wardrobes. Four males: curly-haired outdoor types with above-average table manners. A nice suburban home with a well-manicured lawn. Dad works as an architect but still manages to be home on time for dinner most nights.

In just 30 minutes, this televised blended family encounters a conflict, resolves it successfully (usually with pooled wisdom from the three intelligent adults in the household), then smiles for the camera, sailing confidently into the future. Blending a family never looked simpler or more inviting.

WHEREVER WE GO, PEOPLE TALK to us about *The Brady Bunch.* All of us know and love the show—now it's winning a new generation through continual reruns on cable television. We also know this: Real life isn't much like Brady world!

"How can we make it work like on the Bradys?" is a typical question we hear. Everyone laughs when the question is raised, yet many blended families are wondering the same thing.

"It's simple," we usually respond. "Hire Alice!"

Hiring a housekeeper, even the always calm, always wise Alice, is not the answer to most blended-family stresses. Inviting television cameras into your home is probably not helpful either! Real life in a blended family is a daily struggle. Everyone needs an "attitude check" at some point during the typical day.

Helping a family find unity and strength doesn't involve any magic. Instead, it involves a lot of patience, a lot of gritty persistence, and a lot of hard work on everyone's part. Yet unity as a family is not only possible, it's eventually a likely outcome— once you know how to approach your challenges in a strategic and productive manner.*

In this chapter we'll look at some of the most effective strategies being discovered and used by real-life blended families.

Take the Long View (Keep Things in Perspective)

Never judge your success as a family by what happens on your worst day. Everyone has bad days in a blended family. Many blended families, as they begin to adjust to one another, have a lot more bad days than good ones!

If you're finding it's a struggle to live together peacefully and make wise decisions as a group, welcome to the club. You're normal—your experience is typical of what other blended families are also discovering on a daily basis.

Your task is not to succeed in a few days or to be thriving in a few months. Instead, try to think about your goals within a long-term framework. What kind of family dynamics do you hope to see happening three years from now? How do you picture your family gathering, getting along, and functioning on a daily basis five years from right now? What specific goals

---

* If you find insight in this section, or if you have tips to share from your own experience, we'd love to hear from you! Our e-mail address is included in the biographical information at the close of this book. If you've got a story to share, we're listening!

do you have for each of your children, both your own and your partner's?

When "success" as a family is a short-term goal for you, frustration is likely to follow. Every failure to communicate becomes a crisis. Every small argument requires a full-blown family meeting. It's almost impossible to succeed quickly—trying to do so is an exercise in futility.

A more profitable approach is to choose strategies today that help your family make the slow, gradual transition toward unity. Doing so helps relieve the pressure everyone in the family feels when things aren't working well.

JEFF AND DIANE BLENDED her three kids and his two into a family that fought almost daily during the first six months. At times, they felt they were living a nightmare. Frequently, at the end of the day, the couple honestly admitted to each other that perhaps they'd made a mistake trying to blend.

"We knew that we loved each other, and that helped a lot," Diane says. "But some days that was all we had! Everything else seemed to be going wrong for us. We had terrible financial pressures, the kids seemed to hate each other, and many times they told us we'd made a mistake in getting married."

Had they made a mistake?

Jeff shrugs his shoulders with a resigned smile. "We made a ton of mistakes. Probably one thing we did was try to move too quickly to get married and put our families together. Looking back, we should have waited a little longer. We should have given the kids more chances to be around each other without having to live with each other.

"So we made mistakes. But Diane is right: Our love is the real thing. So after a few months of feeling like total failures, we started to get things sorted out. We sat down one Sunday night after a very horrible weekend, just the two of us, and we kind of planned our attack for the coming week.

"One thing we decided that night was this—we were staying

together, no matter what, and we weren't going to let the kids' fights divide our family. We decided that instead of getting angry, arguing with the kids, and explaining every decision we made, we were just going to ignore most of their outbursts, smile at them if possible, and keep on going forward.

"After a week of trying that, nothing in our family seemed any different. But one reality was totally altered—Diane and I were *so much less stressed out!* It was amazing how much more peaceful we were once we decided to just ignore the yelling and keep moving ahead."

Diane nods. "I started to sleep at night after that. I hadn't really been sleeping well for the whole time we'd been married. I felt guilty for exposing my kids to such a stressful situation. I wondered if I was ruining their lives. But once we decided to stay together, argue with the kids less, smile more often, and just keep staggering forward, everything began to change for the two of us. It took a while, but eventually things started changing for the kids too."

What Jeff and Diane discovered in the heat of battle can be useful to your family before the struggle starts. One common problem faced by remarried couples is the false expectation that blending a family will be relatively easy, just like it seems for Mike and Carol Brady in their 30-minute segments.

Keep your expectations low, however. If anything, expect struggle and difficulty. And instead of trying to succeed in three months, think more in terms of three years, five years, or even a decade. Plan for long-term, not immediate, success.

Finesse It Instead of Forcing It

When *The Mary Tyler Moore Show* ended its long and popular run on network television, the cast gathered on stage for a group hug. As the camera pans back across the cast for the last time, we see everyone huddled together, moving en masse toward the Kleenex box. The cast members have tears in their eyes. Are they acting, or are their true emotions being revealed?

So-called blended families often begin their journeys with a deep desire for a group hug. The parents, who have decided they love each other and want to be married, desperately hope everyone gets along. Typically, these well-meaning parents plan activities they hope will bring the new family together into a cohesive and well-adjusted unit—right away.

The Mary Tyler Moore Show could not have ended with a group hug after just a few episodes. One reason the hug and the tears seemed so believable, seemed to transcend television and speak to a reality among the corps of actors, is that the group had been with each other for a long time. They'd been through a lot together—a lot of shared experiences, a lot of changing seasons. They'd been through highs and lows and transitions in between. They'd seen success, and they'd also known some failure.

It takes a lot of experience together as a group—or else a deeply traumatic experience—before that kind of bonding becomes spontaneous, heartfelt, and universal.

It is much the same way with blended families. It is completely unrealistic to expect a group of children—children whose lives have already been affected negatively by death or divorce and by the breakup of their previous family unit—to immediately like each other, get along well together, and start singing "Kum Ba Yah" for family devotions on the first night.

That task would be impossible for a group of reasonably well-adjusted adults; it's absurd to expect it of insecure, immature adolescents and children. Into the midst of their chaos you are already introducing yet more change just by getting remarried. The kids will make adjustments better if they can make them at a pace that is realistic and useful. That pace, as you need to know, will be slow.

Your task as a parent is to finesse the unity, rather than forcing it. When the family has a positive experience together, notice what's happening and call attention to it. When you accidentally discover something that's working, make note of your strategy and put it to good use. Meanwhile, relax about all the ways in which your family doesn't seem to be bonding. You're probably all doing a lot better than you think you are!

When Quentin married Darcy, she was caring for three children, the oldest two of whom were adolescent girls. Both adults deeply hoped that the two girls would quickly bond with the new man in the house, forming a union that would be affectionate, caring, and supportive. Instead, both girls seemed indifferent to Quentin, rejecting his best efforts to spend time with them.

Darcy was deeply disappointed, and she found herself angry with the girls, ready to yell at them for their continued withdrawal and apathy. But before she sat them down and began to give instruction, she had a brief chat with Quentin over a cup of coffee.

"Maybe I'm just trying too hard," Quentin wondered aloud. "Maybe if I back off a little bit and wait, they'll eventually come to *me*."

Darcy wasn't convinced. She still wanted to criticize her daughters for their obvious indifference and rudeness.

Quentin asked her to hold off for a while. "Give me some time to try this new approach. Whatever happens, it can't be any worse than the silent treatment and rejection I'm already getting from them."

To Darcy's surprise, the strategy worked. Quentin began investing more time in her son, who warmly received the attention and returned the affection. The relationship between the two males bloomed into a genuine partnership of common interests.

In less than a month, Darcy's daughters spoke up. "Why doesn't Quentin ever spend time with us?" they asked their mother one rainy afternoon. "Why does Caleb get all of his time and attention?"

Darcy was wise enough not to blurt out what she was really thinking.

"Would you like to spend more time with Quentin?" she asked the girls.

"We'd love that!" they both responded.

What had happened in a month or so to bring about the change?

"I haven't got a clue," Quentin confides. "I just got tired of being rejected, and I decided to invest my emotional energy somewhere else. I don't know why that worked, or why the girls suddenly decided to be nice to me, but somehow ignoring them brought them around!"

Darcy agrees. "We didn't change anything about how we behaved," she explains. "We kept everything the same, except Quentin quit trying to do things with the girls and spent tons of time doing things with my son. After about a month of that, the girls got jealous of their brother and wanted some attention of their own!"

Finesse—not force.

OTHER REMARRIED COUPLES RELATE similar stories. The common theme is that once the new partner or new family member quits working so hard to achieve a bond with the family, everything starts to work out much better overall.

Is trying too hard a problem?

"It was for me," Sharon confides. "When I married Denny, I immediately started preparing these elaborate meals for his family, keeping the house neat as a pin, baking cookies in the afternoon—anything I thought a supermom would probably be doing. I was exhausted! And no matter how hard I worked, his kids didn't say thanks and didn't stop to compliment me on anything I was doing.

"One afternoon in the kitchen, experimenting with a new recipe, I just mentally said 'to heck with it all' and quit trying so hard," she continues. "I let the house get messy, and I started making macaroni and cheese from a box.

"After a few weeks of that, the children were noticeably nicer to me. I wasn't doing anything differently towards them—I was just working a lot less on all the supermom chores.

"For the life of me, I can't understand why doing *less* brought me more rewards from my new husband's kids. But that's exactly how things worked out."

Children of divorce typically have a lot of displaced anger to deal with. Although it's unfair and also not justified, the newest member of the family—stepdad or stepmom—often receives the brunt of this displaced anger, perhaps as outright rebellion or often as sullen withdrawal.

Instead of fighting that reality it may be wiser to ignore it. Find what succeeds, give attention where it's welcomed, work hard where it produces obvious results. When strategies don't bear fruit, relax and move on. In general, trying too hard is likely to bring about the exact opposite of the reaction you hope for from children, particularly with teens and adolescents.

Does it seem like your new partner's teens don't like you? Deal with it. Be polite to them, but don't go out of your way trying to win them over. Relax, focus on the positives, and wait for time to pass. Waiting appears to work a lot more effectively than trying too hard.

Learn to Celebrate What Is

If there is any one strategy blended families need to master, it is this: learning to celebrate things the way they are.

Blended families exist in the first place because of brokenness, loss, pain, and emotional or physical suffering. They often come into being because of promises not kept, commitments abandoned, and loyalties shattered.

Against this backdrop of grief and mourning, or perhaps because of it, blended families often strive for a "perfect" experience. Let's face it—there is no such thing! And if there were, blended families would be noticeably at a disadvantage in working toward it.

Instead of always striving toward an imaginary perfection, blended families would be well served by learning to celebrate reality just as it is.

In one of the most unusual stories we've heard, a mother told us about her daughter's behavior after she and her husband had divorced. In subsequent years, on the day of the divorce, the teen daughter wore black clothing, including a prominent black armband—not her normal manner of dress.

When the mother inquired about it, her daughter explained herself. "Oh, today is D-day," the daughter said. "As in Divorce Day." The daughter acted out her anger and pain by wearing black on the anniversary of her parents' divorce. She continued to do so each year.

The mother, who was the custodial parent, was unnerved by this behavior but did not ban it. Several years later, she remarried. She happened to share the daughter's "D-Day" concept with her new husband a few days before the anniversary.

When "D-Day" dawned, the new husband appeared dressed in black, including a black armband. The daughter looked at him strangely during breakfast but said nothing as he headed off to work, still dressed in black.

Not until later, after family dinnertime, did the daughter make a comment on the subject.

"Why did you wear black today?" she challenged her stepdad.

"It's D-Day," he responded quietly, "the day your parents got divorced." His tone and manner made it clear he was not mocking her; he was joining the mourning, recognizing it as true grief.

"I didn't know what to expect. I half expected her to be angry at me for stealing her way of expressing things," the stepdad recalls. "What really happened was the last thing I ever expected—when I identified with her pain, she decided to open up and trust me with her feelings."

For the next six hours, until after three o'clock in the morning, the angry daughter of divorce and the new husband in the household shared a conversation that was deep, meaningful, and memorable. Tears were shed on both sides. The outcome was a bond between stepdad and stepdaughter that is strong to this day.

There are no magic formulas in step-parenting; what worked in this case might completely backfire in a similar situation. Somehow, the stepdad in this family unit managed to communicate his empathy and concern with genuineness and sincerity. His participation in his stepdaughter's very real pain prompted her to open up and let him into her world. Instead of attacking the daughter's manner of expression, as the mother had been tempted to try, the stepdad intuitively realized that her pain should be treated with respect. For this adolescent girl, the day of her parent's divorce was a day of celebration—in a mournful, sorrowing way.

The stepdad joined in the celebration of mourning; the result was the beginning of a deep and meaningful relationship.

More typically, celebrating things as they are means being glad about what you gain as a new family instead of being sad about what you've lost. Sadness comes easily enough without any help—gladness is a conscious choice.

Finding the joy in being a new family can be as simple as noticing when someone gets a good grade, partying when a soccer game is won, or having a family minivacation when a parent gets a raise or a good review at work. Since good things are happening all around you, spend some time discovering those things and calling attention to them. Celebrate and affirm the joys of your life.

Pain will find you when you least expect it. In spite of that, or perhaps because of it, make a conscious effort to celebrate, affirm, and share the blessings and delights that come to you as a blended family.

Building New Traditions

One of the most powerful unifying activities in any family unit is the development of shared traditions. These may begin as something small and seemingly trivial, yet over time these same traditions take on a life of their own. Later, looking back at life, they may produce some of the most memorable times spent together as a family.

To a blended family, each partner may bring traditions that worked in a prior household, hoping perhaps to continue the tradition in the new family. This has worked in some cases. It has backfired miserably in others. In general, before trying to impose a previous tradition on a newly blended family, talk about it very openly with the family members who are new. If it doesn't seem as meaningful or useful to those family members, and particularly to the new adult, it may be wisest to let the tradition be a memory of the former family.

Find new traditions as a way of affirming the new family being formed. Among the traditions we've heard about in blended families, what follows are some of the most interesting and unusual. Use these as starting places as you creatively invent your own traditions. Or shamelessly borrow some of these and adapt them to become your own. In any event, look for ways to build traditions into the life of your new family. Over time, the power of traditions may unify you and provide some positive memories to mix in with the difficult ones.

Bathrobe Caroling

One blended family celebrates a Christmas Eve tradition that seems unusual, to say the least. They borrowed the idea from a youth pastor who led his teen group in a similar activity.

On Christmas Eve, the family dresses up in their warmest

clothing (they live in a colder state), including overcoats, hats, mittens, and scarves. Then, they wrap warm bathrobes around themselves—on top of all their other layers.

"We all look like Frosty the Snowman," says the dad about their winter gear. "It's not exactly a figure-flattering look for any of us!"

The roly-poly family then jumps into their minivan and circulates among the houses of friends from church they know will be home. They ring the doorbell and then sing one or two Christmas carols on the porch.

"We've done it three years in a row, and we're starting to get requests," the dad laughs. "This past year we had several families asking us in advance to come over and sing to them in our bathrobes."

Like many traditions, this one met with initial resistance, especially from the two older children, who were teens. Yet also like many traditions, the people who most opposed it at first are now among the strongest proponents of the idea.

The teen daughter of the home, who greatly objected to the bathrobe caroling idea when it was presented, now carries it to extremes—wearing curlers in her hair and a shower cap on her head.

"We're going bathrobe caroling again, aren't we?" she asked a few weeks ahead of this year's event. She then went to a Goodwill store in the area and purchased what she termed "the most hideous" bathrobe she could find.

"Take a picture of me!" she insisted before the carolers departed this year.

Good traditions are like that.

The Soup Kitchen

Another blended family volunteers at a soup kitchen every Thanksgiving.

"I'll tell you a secret," the mother confides during our interview. "This didn't start out as such a holy idea. The truth is, I just got tired of all the cooking and all the dishes and all the hassle. So I thought, *Why don't we find a way to serve others?* But honestly, I enjoy not having to do all that baking!"

On Thanksgiving Day, instead of eating a huge meal and watching a football game on television, the family arrives at a homeless shelter around 9 AM and spends the morning helping prepare a hearty lunch. Then for about three hours during the middle portion of the day, they serve a hot meal to homeless people.

"When you see homeless people out on the street in cold weather, lining up to eat a meal you're about to serve them—all of a sudden, you realize you don't have any problems at all," says B.J., age 15. "It kind of puts things in focus about how rich we are, and how much stuff we have."

At the end of a long day serving others, the family cleans up and goes out to Denny's together. "I usually get a turkey *sandwich,* at least," says the father, smiling. "But the kids are more likely to order Mexican food or maybe pizza. Their whole idea of Thanksgiving doesn't revolve around turkeys and football, it revolves around serving people who have worn-out clothes and holes in their shoes."

Good traditions are like that.

The Outlet Mall

One blended family's tradition involves going to an outlet mall on the day after Christmas. The tradition has evolved and been refined over time.

"We didn't really start it as a tradition," the mom admits. "Actually, one Christmas things were even tighter than normal. Instead of giving gifts to the kids, we promised them a small amount of money to shop with on the day after Christmas. And in thinking about it that year, we decided the money would go further at the outlet mall—so that's where we went."

Intended as a one-year compensation for being so poor, the

event has become an annual tradition the whole family antici-
pates.

"We give everyone a set budget," the father reports. "The
adults, the kids, everyone gets the same fixed amount of money.
We have set rules, and we require receipts. No one can spend
more than the amount we budget, even if they've got money
saved up from during the year!"

No one remembers exactly how the tradition became a con-
test.

"Somehow, it's become a game for us," the father continues.
"All of us compete to see who can get the highest dollar amount
(retail price) for the budget that we're on. The winner doesn't
get anything—except of course the undying respect of the rest
of us—but it's really fun to watch how hard everyone tries to
get the most dollar value."

Good traditions are like that.

The Camping Trip

"Nobody wanted to go," is how the mother remembers the
original experience. "It had rained all week, the weather was terrible, and it seemed like the worst possible time to go camping."

Bravely, because they'd already decided on their plan and
reserved a spot at a state park, the newly blended family ven-
tured out for their first adventure together as a household.

"We set up the tent in the rain," the father recalls. "I was
yelling at people telling them where the tools were, what I
needed next…"

It hardly sounds like an auspicious beginning.

"I cooked our first meal (a spaghetti dinner) in pouring
rain," the mother remembers. "The sauce was a little thinner
than I might have planned."

The worst imaginable weather made for a most memorable
trip.

"It stormed all night," the father recounts. "Booming

thunder, wind blowing the sides of the tent in around us, lightning flashing in the sky. I don't think any of us really slept, but the point is—we survived.

"Sometime in the middle of the night, the storm must have died out. We woke up to sunshine and birds singing and a perfect campsite right at lake's edge. Of course the ground was wet and the world was a soggy place, but it was sunny and beautiful that morning as we made breakfast. And the rest of the weekend, the weather was perfect.

"What's funny," he continues, "is that none of us ever bothers to remember the perfect weather. When we talk about that very first trip, and we do, we talk about the storm that night, how scared we were, and how wet we all got. That storm gets worse with every passing year!"

Intended as a one-time bonding experience, the camping trip has become an annual tradition on the same weekend: Labor Day. And the children who most opposed the idea on the original occasion are among the biggest fans today.

Good traditions are like that.

As you can see from the above stories, blended family traditions don't have to start out well, don't have to succeed quickly, and don't have to be popular from the beginning. Somehow, making the effort has the power to get things moving in a positive direction—even if a little rain dampens the occasion.

Your family may not be a camping family, and this year's budget may not allow for even a one-time trip to an outlet mall. (At the very least, however, you probably do own some "hideous" bathrobes!) The point is, find a tradition that fits your own identity and reality as a family.

If you try a few ideas that fizzle and die, keep trying. Sooner or later you'll encounter a moment that exceeds what you were hoping for and becomes larger than life in the retelling. That's how you'll know you've succeeded.

And when the teens or the children who groaned the most,

protested the loudest, and invented the most excuses for avoiding the occasion suddenly become the proudest defenders of your new tradition, you'll know you're doing at least *something right* as a blended family.

Good traditions are like that.

CHAPTER TEN

The "X" Factor

Strategies for Dealing with Your Former Spouse

❄

*Husbands and wives were
meant to be together forever.
Any time "forever" falls apart,
things can get pretty messy.*

JANET WAS READY TO SCREAM.

For the third Friday in a row, her ex-husband was late to pick up the kids for the weekend. Again, she was back on the cell phone, rescheduling appointments and making apologies for being late. This had to stop!

Before she had gotten remarried, he had been relatively easy to deal with. Not that things were simple—they rarely were. But she could count on him to do what he said he would do. He was usually on time for their exchanges of children on the weekends. He generally behaved like a responsible adult.

Not any more. Since the remarriage, her ex had been acting badly. If he said he would pick up the kids at 3 PM on Friday, it might mean 5 PM or even 8 PM. When he said he would call the next day, he rarely did so.

Janet was at wit's end. Her family life and her business relationships required her to make appointments and to keep them.

But her ex-husband's immature and irresponsible behavior was harming Janet's rapport with her customers.

Frustrated and angry, she turned to a professional counselor for advice. She made no effort to involve her ex-husband—somehow she realized she was going to have find the tools she needed to survive, all by herself.

Have you found yourself in a situation like Janet's? When a divorced person remarries, the relationship with the ex-partner often changes for the worse. Although the ex-spouse may express his support for the new union, his behavior may tell a different story. All types of acting out and behaving badly can and do occur.

In rare cases, the relationship between divorced persons improves and flourishes after a remarriage. More typically, there is a period of adjustment during which the relationship deteriorates, reverting to a state much more similar to that of the immediate aftermath of the divorce. All the progress that has been made in handling issues of child care and finances may suddenly evaporate. Life may get more difficult just when you expected things to simplify themselves.

If you find yourself in such a situation, don't be surprised. Take positive and proactive steps to deal with the problems you may encounter, and be calm and reasonable when your ex-partner is unable or unwilling to do the same.

Be the Grown-Up

Divorce has a way of reversing the maturity levels of some people who suffer through it. Long-accomplished progress in controlling emotions and behaving responsibly can vanish overnight. Long-suppressed angers and resentments can come bubbling to the surface, expressing themselves in inappropriate ways.

Divorce puts some of us right back in middle school again—entangled in a web of complicated and difficult relationships, besieged by changing loyalties, and burdened with emotional pain. We recognize we're not quite as professional, not quite as mature, and not quite as responsible as we believed we were.

Among its other outcomes, divorce shatters our self-delusions. As we adjust to the new realities of life after divorce, adult maturity begins to slowly reassert itself in our behavior patterns. We make and keep schedules. We incur financial obligations and honor them. We experience slow but definite progress toward becoming well-adjusted members of society again.

When a partner remarries, our emotions may surprise us. Even though we tell ourselves we've moved on, having closed that chapter in our lives forever, we may be astonished at the depth of the feelings that surface within us. Suddenly, for no good or obvious reason, we're jealous or petty or resentful.

Some of us transfer those feelings into immature and unstable behaviors, making life difficult for those around us and causing hardships for ourselves. Some of us act out our worst impulses and our basest emotions. Some of us say and do things that cause us shame and regret; others say and do the same things but seem impervious to the pain and suffering they inflict on others.

It's normal to experience mixed emotions when a partner remarries. Evidence suggests that mixed emotions may even be typical throughout the whole context of a remarriage, or at least through a large number of years as the new relationship evolves and establishes itself. Having unresolved or ambivalent feelings is not only natural, it's also extremely common. It's normal.

In the midst of the confusion and adjustment, someone has to step up to the plate and behave like an adult. Someone has to become or remain responsible, act with a measure of authority, and function wisely amid the challenges.

Let that someone be you. Difficult as it is, impossible as it may seem, you can function responsibly even when your emotions are complicated and frustrating. Life begins to get better when someone musters the courage and finds the emotional resources to behave in a mature and reasonable way.

Janet's counselor showed her what the next steps might look like. Since her ex-husband was perpetually late to pick up their children, the counselor advised her to find a way to keep her own appointments—regardless of whether or not her ex-husband was timely and prompt in keeping his.

This meant one of two courses of action. Either Janet could take the children along with her to her appointments, keeping to her schedule as planned, or she could arrange for backup child care, bringing in a relative or sitter to care for the children until her former spouse finally arrived.

Although difficult and potentially expensive, either of these choices allowed her to keep her own commitments and adhere to her own schedule, rather than allowing her ex-husband to damage her business and social life.

Janet chose the first option, though it meant not only bringing the children along but also transporting their backpacks and other gear, since they would be spending the weekend with their father and his live-in girlfriend. It also meant she would have to attempt to do business while juggling the children. How did this choice work out?

"The first time I tried it, I didn't tell my ex where we would be," Janet says with an ironic smile. "That was probably childish of me, but by then I was angry anyway and didn't really care. I allowed him 20 minutes to arrive at our house and pick up the kids. When he didn't show up, I just threw all their gear into the car and drove them to my appointment as planned. My ex eventually showed up at the house, couldn't find any of us, and called on the cell to ask where we were.

"I told him exactly where we were. I also told him how long we'd be there. I made it clear we weren't going to wait for him at this location or at any other place. If he didn't get here before my appointment ended, we'd be off to the next one—not waiting around for him to show up.

"Well, he made it, with maybe five minutes to spare. I had finished with my client by then so I was able to talk to him briefly. I told him I would no longer be waiting for him when it was time to pick up the kids. I told him that if, on some rare occasion, he was running a little late, he should call me to find out where the kids would be.

"He was surprised but didn't say anything. However, the next week he was actually on time to pick up the kids—well, ten minutes late, which is 'on time' for him. And since then he's been consistently on time (ten minutes late), and I've just built those ten minutes into my schedule."

With the counselor's help, Janet began functioning like a grown-up. Since she had made appointments with clients who expected her to appear, she began to keep those appointments rather than allowing her ex-husband's immaturity to ruin her business relationships. Her stress level began to decrease immediately.

Her actions expressed appropriate authority in dealing with another adult. If her ex-husband could not keep to his agreed schedule, there would be consequences—the kids would be at another location. The imposition of consequences had the effect of "maturing" him, at least with regard to his timeliness in picking up his children for the weekend.

You should not expect your own adult behavior to automatically transform the behavioral patterns of your ex-partner. Instead, the world you are attempting to transform is your own. Janet's counselor was not intentionally devising a way to produce responsible behavior in her ex-husband; rather, she aimed at helping Janet keep her own commitments, maintain her thriving business, and experience less stress while doing so.

Janet kept seeing the counselor for a while and worked on some other issues as well. The result was that she was able to retain her self-respect and her dignity while coping with an immature ex-spouse and making the many adjustments that her new marriage required.

In a world of immature attitudes and juvenile behaviors, someone has to be the grown-up. Make the choice to let that someone be you.

Keep Calm, and at Least Be Polite

When one person begins to behave badly, other affected persons may want to retaliate. At the very least, they may choose to vent their anger and frustration, yelling at or arguing with the offending party.

This is normal, but it usually doesn't improve the situation or resolve the problem. Instead, reacting this way usually escalates the warfare to a new level.

When you respond to bad behavior by behaving badly yourself, you inherit a universe that isn't much fun to live in. Regardless of what the other person may experience emotionally, you will probably find yourself with elevated levels of stress and anxiety—and with feelings that are perpetually upset.

Fortunately, there is another way to live. "Love your enemies, do good to those who hate you, bless those who curse you, and pray for those who mistreat you," Jesus tells His followers in His famous Sermon on the Mount (Luke 6:27-28). While, hopefully, we need not think of our ex-spouses as enemies, it is entirely possible that our ex-partners will curse us, hate us, and mistreat us.

The counsel of Christ is clear on this matter: We should do our best not to pay them back in the same way. Living as Christ counseled may not bring about world peace, yet it does have the power to transform our inner world, bringing us internal serenity.

It takes two to fight, as the old adage explains. In other words, by keeping ourselves calm in the midst of frustrating situations, we can prevent the development of a full-blown argument or an all-out confrontation. Doing so is incredibly difficult but is entirely possible.

SHEILA IS LIVING PROOF. "After I remarried, things went downhill with my ex really fast," she remembers. "I didn't understand why, and I still don't. All I know is he started fighting with me about almost everything. Even things we had already agreed to were suddenly up for grabs. Everything was an argument with him!"

In all probability, Sheila's ex-husband found himself jealous about her remarriage. More than likely, he became angry as he thought about her getting married to another man. By provoking arguments with her and picking fights, he gave himself a good excuse to yell, scream, and argue—finding a way to displace his anger by venting it on his ex-spouse.

Sheila responded by being angry in return. "I had remarried—he hadn't. Our fights after I got remarried were a lot worse than our fights when we were married or even our fights after we got divorced!"

Sheila grew tired of the fighting and decided to talk with her minister. Patiently and with good humor, he explained Christ's counsel.

"There was no way I wanted to be kind to my ex," she admits. "He was being a complete jerk, and I enjoyed telling him so. But I was tired of all the fighting, and I was worried it might start affecting our kids. So I was open to what the pastor told me, even though I didn't like the advice one bit when I first heard it."

Sheila asked two women in her church to pray for her, that she would learn to hold her tongue when dealing with her ex-husband rather than being drawn into arguing and fighting.

How did this strategy work out?

"Not very well, at first," Sheila says candidly. "I found out that I'm not very good at staying calm when someone is yelling at me. The first few times I tried it, I had to call those two women and apologize—they had prayed for me, but I had totally let them down—I wasn't nice to my ex at all. I yelled back!

"I was shocked when both women told me not to worry about it, that God would help me get better. I didn't expect them to react like that. Maybe I thought if I failed to do the right thing, I could get off the hook."

Sheila kept trying, the women kept praying, and things improved.

"My ex is still a jerk," she says with a loud laugh. "But thank God, I've really gotten better at not fighting. It's been a long time since we had a big blowout with yelling and screaming. Nowadays when my ex tries that, God helps me to keep my cool, respond in a kind way, and avoid a big fight."

Among the wise decisions Sheila made was to seek support in prayer and to find a way to be accountable. She not only formed deep relationships with the women who were praying for her, she also found herself transformed by being able to tell someone the truth about what was really going on.

If you're truly unable to stay calm with your ex despite your best efforts, then at least try to be polite. Don't let yourself be baited into trading insults or attacking. Shut your mouth, stifle your impulses, do everything possible to avoid being drawn into an argument. Force yourself to remain silent even in the midst of a highly upsetting discussion.

Talk with your minister, seek help from a counselor, or ask friends to help you be accountable to them for your choices and behaviors. Since you probably can't change your ex-partner anyway, work on the things that you can control: your own attitudes, your own responses, and your own choices.

As we've noted, among the many advantages of behaving politely is its effect on your own levels of stress and anxiety. After a big fight, although you may have enjoyed the chance to air your feelings, it's typical to find your pulse racing and your breathing shallow. You may feel anxious and upset. The feelings may linger long after the fighting has subsided.

In contrast, after avoiding a fight, you'll notice your pulse is stable and your breathing is controlled. In lieu of the feelings of anxiety, you'll have an increasing quantity of self-respect. Go ahead and be proud of yourself: learning to keep a lid on your emotions is something to take pride in.

No one is asking you to become a doormat, to put up with emotional or verbal abuse, or to allow your ex-partner to get away with unreasonable demands. Rather, the intention of this strategy is to help you remain calm while coping wisely with an ex-partner who may become abusive or unreasonable.

The one who will gain the most is you yourself. In addition, your new partner and your family will also benefit—they'll be in a relationship with a person who is less stressed, less frustrated, and more serene. In fact, everyone around you will benefit from the progress you make in learning how to be calm and polite in the face of adversity and argument.

When the Kids Are Around, Speak Positively

"Does Daddy still love me?" Kayla, age six, asked her mother. She had lived in her mother's custody for five months since the divorce became final.

Janice, Kayla's mom, still regrets her response. "If he loved either one of us, he wouldn't have left us!" she almost shouted at her daughter. She then proceeded to launch a blistering verbal attack against her ex-husband, listing all his many faults.

Years later, remarried and the mother of two children with her new husband, she realizes she made a big mistake with Kayla. "I shouldn't have told her that. I should have told her that her Daddy still loved her, because he did. It was me he didn't love—it was only me he was trying to run away from.

"In my hurt and anger and confusion, I didn't get all that sorted out for a long time. Meanwhile, I shared a lot of anger about Richard while Kayla was growing up. She was old enough to understand my comments about him."

For most of her childhood, and especially as she entered adolescence Kayla was a "problem child," constantly rebelling at school and also at home. She became sexually active at an early age, involving herself with males who tended to be angry, violent, and possessive.

The absence of a stable, positive relationship with their father is increasingly cited as a contributing factor in emotional and behavior problems in adolescent and teen girls. Janice, wiser now, realizes she should never have poisoned her daughter's relationship with her birth dad. Unfortunately, that realization occurred much too late to help Kayla navigate the challenging transition into adult and family life.

She was pregnant at 15. Her mother knows of at least two abortions before Kayla turned 18 and left home for good. Though these days the relationship between mother and daughter is fairly open, it was often stormy and argumentative during middle-school and high-school years.

Although Kayla's birth father made numerous efforts to establish a relationship with his daughter, Janice had poisoned her opinion of her dad, and the two of them never formed a meaningful connection. Rightly or wrongly, Janice continues to see that as her own fault.

"I needed someone else to hate Richard as much as I did, someone to take my side of things, someone to give me sympathy," she says now. "I guess I sort of trained Kayla to be that person, and it worked well when she was little. Then later as she got into her teen years I began to see I had really destroyed her relationship with her dad. I began to see a lot of problems in her life because of that. I wish somebody had told me what I was doing in those early years. Maybe I would have listened."

It can be extremely helpful to find a sympathetic, listening ear as you process the emotional pain of abandonment and divorce. Talking with a close friend, a minister, a counselor, or your new marriage partner can be a healthy, liberating experience that brings you healing and comfort.

However, talking with children about these same issues can cause lasting damage, impairing their ability to move through adolescence and into adulthood with healthy self-images and positive social relationships. Using your own children as counselors may be a comforting choice, but it is not a wise one.

VICKY'S MOTHER WAS a high-school counselor. When Vicky divorced after having two children, her mother had prompt advice. "However you may feel about David," Vicky remembers her mother telling her, "put all that aside when you talk to the kids about him. When you talk to the kids, always tell them that David still loves them, David still cares about them, David still wants to be their daddy and their friend."

At the time, Vicky wasn't particularly grateful for the advice. In fact, she often felt like her mother was meddling in her life in ways that weren't helpful. Only now, looking back, does she realize her mother's wisdom.

"My kids grew up knowing that their mom and their dad both loved them a lot," she says today. "For some reason I followed my mom's advice even though I didn't always appreciate it. I told those kids their daddy loved them very much, and I loved them very much, and even though we lived in two different houses, we would always be one family."

She made a special effort to keep the "one family" theme active and alive as her children were growing up. Today, both of her first two children (she remarried and had children with her new husband) are in their mid-teens. Both have positive and constructive relationships with their birth father, who also has remarried. They bounce back and forth between the two households, seemingly adjusting in good ways to the challenges of their high-school years. Her daughter, who is active in a church youth group, has taken a chastity pledge to keep herself pure until she gets married.

"There's only one problem with that," Vicky says in a moment of complete candor. "Jessica sometimes says she doesn't plan to get married. Even after all these years you can tell the divorce hurt her. It hurt us all! Sometimes I worry she doesn't have a high enough opinion of marriage."

The aftermath of divorce and the effect of divorce on children's views of marriage are powerful reasons to build a strong relationship with your new spouse if you remarry. Although you can never erase the past or remove the impact of a divorce, it is possible to model a loving, committed remarriage relationship in ways that do influence and affect your children's beliefs about marriage and family.

Speaking positively about your ex-partner is another way to contribute to your children's overall health and maturity. Even as you struggle to process your own anger and pain, try to nurture a sense of respect for your former spouse in the minds and hearts of the children the two of you bore together.

You may be the only parent who behaves this way; you may learn from the children that your ex-partner speaks badly about you. Ignore this and choose to behave differently. Build up your ex-partner, be supportive of your ex-partner, and especially make every effort to reassure your children that they are loved by *both* of their birth parents.

If, as time passes, it begins to appear that your ex-partner does *not* love the children, let this be their own discovery rather than the result of toxic, negative comments from you. Speak positively, and raise children who feel as secure as possible even in the midst of their fractured family.

"Ex-Laws" Outlast the Ex

One of the many logistical challenges faced by remarriage families is dealing with the extended family members of former spouses, especially around birthdays or major holidays. Although the marriage has ended, the "family ties" that bind generations together still exist.

In general, this is helpful and positive. Even if your ex-partner appears to have come from a highly dysfunctional family, it's wise to realize your children's grandparents, aunts, uncles, and cousins are still their relatives and still have a valid and vested interest in your children's lives.

Paige has a very good relationship with her ex-husband's parents and other members of his extended family. She was in her early 20s, the mother of two young children, when Marcus abandoned her and began an affair with one of her closest friends.

Throughout the breakup and the uncertainty that followed, Marcus's parents remained very supportive of Paige and her children. They were helpful financially, especially in the early years. When she did choose to remarry about six years after the divorce, his parents gave her and her new husband a very generous, very expensive wedding present.

"I could never have made it without them, and they're not even my parents," she exclaims today. "They helped me through the toughest times, not just financially but also emotionally and spiritually. They never abandoned their son and they never judged him, but they were clearly supportive of me and they were always great with the kids.

"My kids have grown up knowing their grandparents and always having a lot of fun when they're around. My dad was dead when I got married to Marcus, and my mom had remarried and lived in another state, so my kids rarely saw their grandparents on my side of the family. Oma and Opa were their favorite relatives. And those were the parents of the man who abandoned us!"

Paige's new husband, Greg, is comfortable around Marcus's parents, seeming to understand they have played an important and valuable role in the lives of his wife and her children.

"I think Greg loves Oma and Opa as much as the rest of us do now," Paige laughs. "I sometimes think he loves them as much as he loves his own parents. And do you hear what I'm telling you? These people aren't Greg's parents, and they're not my parents either. These are the parents of my *ex-husband!*"

Not everyone has "ex-laws" as generous and loving as the couple who have cared so generously for Paige and her children. Sometimes the demands of the ex-relatives can be burdensome and unwelcome, particularly if grandparents or others always insist on having extended visitations or custody during school holidays or major family events.

WHEN CURT AND LEILA GOT MARRIED, each had children from their prior marriages. Each also had an extensive network of ex-laws who wished to remain involved in the lives, accomplishments, and celebrations of those children.

"It's a juggling act around here." Leila shrugs. Especially at Thanksgiving and Christmas time. It's not just sorting out whether our ex's will have the kids or whether we'll have them, it's also working out how or when or where to let the other relatives have a chance to visit."

Leila, an organizing type, originally tried to chart the visits using a color-coded system on a refrigerator-mounted calendar.

"That lasted about one season and never really worked," she admits.

"Basically we try to be fair with everybody," Curt notes. "And of course that means at one time or another, everybody is mad at us. Everybody thinks somebody else is getting preferential treatment, or a better time slot, or whatever. It's enough to drive a man to drink!"

The two keep working at it in spite of criticism and complaints.

"We want our children to know who their family is, to feel connected to their cousins and everybody else," Leila says. "In my opinion, Curt and I are the ones who really lose out. By the time we get done sharing the kids with everybody who wants them, we don't get enough time with them ourselves!"

Curt's solution to that challenge may be useful for other remarriage couples.

"We've started taking a major one-week vacation just before school starts every year," he says. "It's our way of having 'holiday time' with the kids. We give them gifts during the vacation—not a lot of gifts and not elaborate ones, not like a full-blown Christmas celebration would be. But it's our time to be together as just our own family circle, without juggling all the relatives."

How is it working so far?

"Our only major hassle has been football practice," Curt says, shrugging. "I had to talk to the coach for a long time to be sure Jason could still be on the team and not be penalized in some way. That time before school starts is 'prime time' for the team. But after I explained the problem, the coach ended up being supportive. Jason says he hasn't been hassled about it—the coach seems to truly understand."

From Curt and Leila's perspective, it's a little easier to share the kids with others at Easter, Thanksgiving, Christmas, and other holidays when their own family has had a major celebration during their annual vacation.

BE AS GENEROUS AND THOUGHTFUL with your ex-laws as possible. However, don't feel a need to appease them at any price or give in to any unreasonable demands. Some people will push you as far as you can be pushed, so decide for yourself how accommodating and sharing you wish to be.

As much as possible, avoid any sense of competition between different sets of relatives. Let all of the ex-laws know you support and appreciate their interest in your children. Teach your children to send personal thank-you notes; their kindness will stand out in a world increasingly devoid of good manners (and perhaps uninterested in developing them). Particularly with older children, who may be curious about their heritage in biological ways, sit down with a family tree and explain the generations and the connections and the relationships.

You are not the first remarried family required to cope with ex-relatives, and you won't be the last. Compare notes with others and learn from their ideas and experiences. When you discover good ideas from your own efforts, share those with other remarriage families that you know.

If it takes a village to raise a child, the children of remarriage families may be a few steps ahead of the rest. The extended family networks created by divorce and remarriage may produce enough relatives to populate a small village! Instead of lamenting this fact, let it work for your good and for the benefit of the children.

Think inclusively and act generously; your children's lives may be richer and more complete because of their many ex-laws.

CHAPTER ELEVEN

For Poor
or Poorer

Strategies for Dealing with Financial Realities

❄

A remarriage is the combining of
two existing poverties into
a new community of deeper poverty.

T WAS THE ONE CONVERSATION Ray was dreading the most. He and Debbie had dated steadily for almost a year. His kids seemed to love her; they seemed to like her young daughter also. Her daughter appeared to trust and like Ray, and she seemed happy about gaining new siblings.

The two families had done a lot together: grocery shopping, fast food, renting movies on DVD from a corner store. They had ordered pizza together for home delivery; they had cooked meals together at Ray's place or at Debbie's. Everything was going great. Ray and Debbie had been talking openly about getting married. Their children seemed relaxed about it.

Sooner or later though, Ray knew he'd have to have "the conversation" about financial realities. He was dreading that—how could he possibly tell Debbie he was not only poor, he was profoundly in debt?

Debbie, unknown to Ray, was dreading the same conversation.

She had tried so hard to appear financially independent, to not seem worried about the high cost of raising her family. In reality, she was borrowing more and more money every month while trying to keep the kids in decent clothes, dental work, and school supplies. She felt like she was drowning in a sea of financial irresponsibility, even though she was genuinely trying to keep a balanced budget and live within her income. Somehow, she just couldn't make it all fit!

It was Ray who first broke the ice, beginning by telling Debbie that he needed to talk to her about money. Something about the way he said it made Debbie aware of how emotional this topic was for him. She tried to prepare herself for whatever she might hear.

For the next couple of hours, the couple told each other the truth about their finances…mostly. Both of them tended to underplay their sense of absolute failure and frustration. Yet both of them readily admitted to things being "difficult"—or, as Debbie phrased it, "out of control."

"I was so relieved," is how she remembers the result of that evening's discussion. "Once I told him how things really were with us, it seemed like a giant load had been lifted off my shoulders."

Ray had a similar feeling. "She was so understanding about it. I expected her to be disappointed and upset. I expected to lose her respect once I admitted I wasn't managing things very well. But instead, she told me she loved me and believed in me, and she knew everything would work out!"

Everything did work out, in a massively impoverished sort of way. Ray and Debbie spent the first three years of their remarriage making monthly choices about which bills to pay and which to postpone. It was a living nightmare. Both realized financial counseling was probably a wise way to proceed, yet neither one wanted to share their true financial condition with a complete stranger.

Working slowly but steadily, they made progress those first three years, yet their credit rating remained low. After three years Ray got a promotion to a better-paying job with the same company, and things improved significantly.

Today, eight years after their remarriage, the couple is debt-free—and enjoying it immensely. "We had a family party," Debbie says about the day their last debt was paid off. "We went out for a great meal at a nice restaurant—and yes, we paid cash for the meal!"

RAY AND DEBBIE'S CASE MAY NOT be typical, but it is not unusual. Many couples remarry under a heavy burden of debt and spend years attempting to become debt-free.

Divorced dads face alimony and child-support duties, while also trying to have enough money left over to support themselves. Divorced moms may or may not be receiving the funds agreed upon in the settlement. Or they may be receiving the funds intermittently or late, or occasionally instead of regularly.

Remarriage is the combining of two existing poverties into a new community of deeper poverty. When remarried couples talk about the issues that are most problematic for them, money always ranks high on the list.

Differing Priorities

When Oscar married Silvia, both were parents of older teens and young adults. Silvia's two children were in college—one at community college and the other at an expensive university nearby. Oscar's children were in high school—one a senior and the other a sophomore. He was busy helping his oldest child pick a college to attend the following year.

"When Silvia told me how much money she was paying so her daughter could attend Stanford, I couldn't believe it!" Oscar exclaims. "I didn't see how the two of us could possibly afford to keep doing that, not to mention how we would take care of our other three kids. I had a huge problem with that."

Silvia sees things much differently. "I've sacrificed all my life so that Aricela could go to Stanford. Now that she's halfway through, I'm not going to start changing the rules for her. I'm not going to back away from what I promised."

The pair had numerous arguments about money as they remarried and formed a new family. Much of their fighting was about college expenses. In the end, neither would compromise.

"A promise is a promise," Silvia insisted. "And besides, my son is living at home and paying for his own courses at community college. So I'm really getting through this a lot more cheaply than I might have. What if my son had wanted to go to Stanford, too?"

Oscar's view differs. "Right when I was helping my son look for a good school," he says, "Silvia's daughter was taking a huge amount of money out of our family budget. My ability to help my son was being harmed by our huge out-of-pocket expense for her!"

Despite their best efforts, the couple failed to find common ground. Silvia insisted on continuing the support for her daughter; Oscar resented the fact that his own children would be receiving a lot less help when it was their turn.

Although they remained together, the disparity in spending between the two sets of children was a major source of division and stress. As much as possible, they kept their fighting behind closed doors.

To keep peace in the family, Oscar never revealed to his own children the scope of financial help Silvia's daughter was receiving. Inwardly, however, he remained angry about his wife's priorities. "We had four kids between us," he declares. "But there were two different standards for those kids. Silvia's daughter got everything; the rest of the kids got very little—which was all we could afford after paying for Stanford."

Different Patterns of Spending

As is true for original marriages, husbands and wives that join together in a remarriage often bring vastly different styles of spending and saving into the new relationship. One may be a big spender, the other a frugal fanatic.

The difference between a remarriage union and an original one is that by the time a couple joins in a remarriage, the patterns of spending may have already been in place for many years. The children of each household may already have adjusted to the spending style of each custodial parent.

Blending two families into one often involves trying to incorporate two very dissimilar approaches to the use of money. And as with every other choice made by the new couple, the children are watching to see how things are decided.

"Dan spoils those kids," is the opinion of Dan's new wife. "Those kids get anything they want, any time they want it. I'd never do that with my kids—and in fact, I'm *not* doing that with mine. My kids know the value of a dollar and they know they have to earn their allowances by hard work!"

Dan, of course, sees it differently. "My kids have suffered through so much in their lives," he sighs. "If there's any way I can help them have a little fun, if there's any way I can make their lives a little bit easier or less stressful—hey, how do you put a price tag on something like that?"

Price Tags—A Major Part of Any Remarriage

Beyond the expenses of getting married and setting up a new home, there may be young children to provide for, teens that need braces, grown children to send off to college, wedding expenses for the children, or adult children who are hoping to move back "home" to save money for a while.

Rarely do both partners bring a similar spending pattern into the new union. The new couple must find common ground and form reasonable compromises in their use of income.

Deciding how money will be spent is a useful test of their problem-solving and conflict-management skills.

Long before deciding to remarry, persons considering this should look carefully at each other's priorities in spending and patterns in using money. This does not involve judging the other person or finding fault—rather, this is a process of discovery and exploration. This helps you form useful compromises even before you've set up your new household.

Compromising about finances is no simpler than compromising about any other topic; it is also no less important. Couples that bring a unified approach to spending and saving into a remarriage have already rescued themselves from one of the greatest sources of conflict. Their odds of thriving in the new relationship increase exponentially if they have already formed some kind of agreement.

Your Checkbook or Mine?

In our ongoing survey of remarried couples, most report they are choosing to keep separate checking accounts as they form their new family. Most also choose to establish at least one joint account. But they still seem to prefer keeping some of their assets in a separate place.

What explains this particular choice?

"It was simple fear on my part," Faye reports. "When my first marriage broke up, I didn't see it coming and I wasn't prepared. I knew nothing at all about how to manage money, and I had no money to manage!

"After years of being on my own, finally learning how to balance a checkbook and behave responsibly, I wasn't ready to just pass all that control off to someone else. Plus, I was afraid— what if this second marriage ended too? I didn't want to have to fight for my money if we ended up divorcing."

In addition to the fear factor, Faye's comment raises the question of control. Those who have experienced divorce have learned the importance of having some semblance of control over their own financial destiny. This hard-fought-for and hard-earned financial authority is not something that can be easily relinquished. Many remarried partners prefer to allow each other to have a separate account from which to support their children, donate to charities, or provide for other matters that are outside of normal living expenses.

Donna, however, disagrees. "One of the best things about getting married again was that I could get rid of the checkbook," she happily asserts. "Marvin is a lot better with numbers than I am—I couldn't wait to hand him the checkbook and let him balance everything."

Does she miss having the power of the purse?

She laughs. "He gives me anything I ask him for. I guess we have a pretty traditional marriage, even though it's a second marriage for both of us. He runs the family and makes the big decisions, and he manages our money.

"Frankly, I love it this way! Paying my own power bills and my own phone bills was never something I learned to enjoy. Who needs the hassle? Marvin pays all our bills, does our taxes, everything. I get to do what I love—take care of the kids, oversee our house, be the chauffeur. I have a credit card for gas and groceries, and guess what—I don't even have to look at the statement when it arrives! If Marvin doesn't understand something on the bill, he'll ask me about it. Usually, everything's clear."

Did Donna and Marvin work this out before they remarried, or after?

"Before," Donna reports. "In fact, we set up a joint checking account about six months before we actually got married. We were already pooling our money and doing a lot of financial things in common even before the wedding."

GARRETT AND NANCY LIVED TOGETHER for two years before remarrying. Both had been active churchgoers before divorcing;

both fell out of the habit of church attendance when divorce shattered their expectations and hopes.

"We fought a lot about money, even when we were living together," Nancy says today. "So nothing changed in that category when we got remarried. We were arguing a lot before, and we argued a lot after our wedding day."

Have they found a solution?

"Sort of," Nancy says. "We divide the regular expenses and each of us pays half of that, since we both work. After that, it gets complicated. I kind of do whatever I want with my money, and Garrett kind of does whatever he wants with his.

"The problems come up when we go out to dinner or go to a movie, or maybe we go away for the weekend. We're not really angry with each other, but we usually end up arguing about who's going to pay for what."

Do they have a joint checking account?

"Who would carry the checkbook?" Nancy asks. "We'd probably fight about that too. So far we just split the living expenses and each of us pays half out of our own accounts. If there's a better way to do it, we haven't figured it out in our 18 months married or the two years living together before that. Both of us are still too stubborn to let the other person control all the money. Maybe it would be different if only one of us had a job—but we both have good jobs, thank God."

Professional Help

Cathy and Stan knew they'd need help with money if they were going to get married. Stan had been in two marriages already; Cathy in one. Both of them were facing significant financial obstacles even if they remained single.

"Our church had a video seminar with Ron Blue," Stan says. "It was easy to sign up, easy to sit there and watch the videos, and they gave us workbooks we could take home. It kind of took the shame out of needing help with money."

During the weeks of watching the video series, Stan and Cathy looked at each other's workbooks, compared notes, and got fully acquainted with the reality of each other's financial situations. They were surprised to find that their cases were fairly similar—both were facing seemingly insurmountable odds.

"We came out of that series with a lot of hope and with some useful tools to manage our money," Cathy notes. "I don't know what would have happened to us if we hadn't gone through that video series before we remarried. And we almost didn't go to it—because there was a tuition cost for attending. We also talked about only one of us going, to save money. But in the end we paid for both of us, we each got our own course materials, and we each did our own homework.

"By the time we remarried, nothing had changed in our finances, but now we knew what we were going to do and how we were going to do it."

Have things worked out well for the couple?

"We're getting there," says Stan. "Both of us still struggle with money. Mostly we struggle to stay hopeful when everything looks so bleak. But the ideas and concepts we learned from the Ron Blue tapes are really working. We're making some good progress—it's just a little slower than we hoped."

The Expense of Not Getting Help

Martin also found help through his church. He had been married previously before wedding Diana, who was nearly 40 and had always been single. Between the expense of divorcing, the ongoing costs of caring for his children, and a nearly 14-month stint out of work, Martin's financial reality was bleak.

Although he loved Diana, he could not imagine taking on yet another financial burden given his low income and high level of expenses. But when he was talking with a friend at church, the friend recommended a book by Larry Burkett.

"I couldn't afford to buy the book," he admits. "But the more

I talked to my friend, the more I decided I couldn't afford *not* to buy it."

Using the principles outlined in the book, Martin was able to produce a comprehensive snapshot of his overall financial reality. To his surprise, things were not as dismal as he had always believed. Further, the book proposed some specific ideas that made a lot of sense to a divorced father of three.

"The money I spent on that book was maybe the best investment I've ever made," he says today. "That book helped me get my financial life turned around and working better. Having my financial life mostly in order helped me find the courage to propose to Diana."

Martin shakes his head. "And what are the odds that right when I needed it, our church bookstore would feature a great book on finances? Does God love me, or what?" he wonders aloud.

Help from Unexpected Places

Keshia and Bryce found help from a surprising source: a real-estate agent.

Bryce begins the story. "We met a couple at church who was involved in real estate. They were in a small group with us, and we found out they sold real estate. As we got to know them a little better, they seemed like they really had a handle on financial stuff. They looked like who we wanted to be, moneywise.

"After our group meeting one night, we asked if we could get together with them to talk about money," he continues. "They looked a little surprised, but they happily agreed. They even ended up inviting us over to their house to talk about things, which was really nice of them."

Over a leisurely meal Bryce and Keshia asked many questions and revealed quite a bit about their financial struggles as a recently remarried couple. The more they chose to reveal, the easier it became to just open up and share the truth with the couple from church.

"We still haven't bought a house from them," Keshia laughs. "And who knows when we'll be able to buy a house? But they didn't care about that. They really wanted to help us get a handle on our finances, and they've done that. They ended up inviting us back over for dinner two more times just to talk more about money. They explained what they do, how things work for them. For one thing, they're really big on tithing, and we weren't doing that since both of us were so poor after our divorces and getting remarried."

Bryce credits the couple with turning his financial situation around. "I was really struggling. I had made a mess of my financial life, then I got remarried. I felt like I was dragging Keshia into the pit with me, month after month. Things were bad. After talking to our friends, I knew what I needed to do, and I started trying to do it. The amazing thing is, it really works."

Other remarried couples have chosen to consult financial professionals such as tax preparers, CPAs, or credit counseling services. The common theme is that professional help from an outside source is highly useful in getting a handle on financial reality. Beyond that, professional help is useful in structuring changes in the way money is earned, saved, and spent. And as is the case with other issues, talking with a neutral third party about an area of struggle in your remarriage is often a highly practical method of finding your way to a workable compromise.

Prenuptial Agreements

The escalation of divorce and remarriage within our culture has prompted a similar escalation in the number of couples who remarry using a carefully defined prenuptial agreement. These documents may pertain only to specific issues such as the custody of children, or they may also specify the eventual financial outcome of any future divorce.

"It was probably the least valuable thing we did before remarrying" is how Samantha characterizes the experience. "We went to an attorney to get new wills drawn up for each of us. From that beginning, things evolved into a full-blown prenuptial agreement.

"What we wanted to be sure of was what would happen to our kids if either of us died or if we got divorced. They were very young, and we were each the primary caregivers. We wanted some kind of legal protection for the children, especially if one of us died right away."

Does Samantha recommend this strategy for other remarried couples?

"It was definitely unromantic," she says. "Looking at everything in black-and-white, thinking about everything from a bottom-line standpoint, that's not a very romantic thing to do. But I would recommend that people think about death and dying, and that people make sure they have a valid, enforceable will. Especially when you get remarried, custody could get messy if you died, so it's important to sit down with a lawyer and set up a professional plan."

Has anything changed since the prenuptial agreement was made?

"I think, if we're still together ten years from now—and we will be—we may go back and undo some of the things we set up," Samantha reflects. "We were both focused on protecting our own children more than anything else. Now that we're becoming a viable family—we have a strong relationship—we don't need all the protections we put in place.

"I'd like to see us sit down in a decade or so, with the kids a lot older, and draw up the kind of will a normal family might make in an original marriage. I really hope our relationship works out like that—and so far it is."

Realistic—But Hopeful for the Future

It's not unusual for one or both spouses to experience times of depression shortly after remarrying. There's a nearly universal reaction of "What have I done?" that tends to set in after a remarriage is finalized.

Often the depression is triggered by a growing awareness of the sizeable financial challenges to face. After the honeymoon phase of the relationship begins to ebb, a bleak sense of despair may descend seemingly overnight. The one who is depressed may not be able to identify the source of the vague feelings of unrest or uneasiness being experienced. Yet at its root, much of the problem will stem from a sense of hopelessness about financial realities.

The task of a remarried couple is to be realistic about money matters—yet also be hopeful about the future. With enough hope, almost any obstacle can be squarely faced, and strategies be derived for attacking the problem. Without hope, almost any obstacle can seem impossible to confront, leading one or both partners to seek escape rather than dealing with reality.

One aspect of reality is this: Rarely does a remarriage itself complicate or worsen the financial picture. Rather, most of the stress about money is directly related to the consequences of divorce and the breakup of the original marriage and family. Simply stated, even without remarrying, most of the financial stresses would still be in place, because they are rooted in the past rather than current decisions.

Whenever possible, capable financial counseling should precede any decision to remarry. If you have remarried without getting advance help, then move as quickly as possible to get any financial advice needed.

Good Reasons for Hope

There is every reason to be hopeful about your financial status as a remarried couple. Just as two persons can literally live more cheaply than one, so also it is often possible for two combined families to live more cheaply than one. Instead of two separate housing expenses, whether rent or mortgage payments, a remarriage family now has only one housing expense. Instead of two sets of utility payments, property taxes, cable television fees, and so on, there is now only one.

It is usually possible for a combined household to spend less money on groceries than the total previously spent by two separate households. Remarried families also tend to economize on luxuries like dining out—this fact by itself begins to help the cash flow of a new family.

If you find yourself irrationally depressed about your finances, it may be wise to seek help from a psychologist or minister. It may well be that your depression is not specifically linked to money at all, but as we've noted before, stems from unresolved issues left over from previous marriages, previous families, and previous pain.

Every day, other remarried couples are coping with exactly the same kinds of financial pressures you are experiencing. Somehow they are finding the courage to start each new day in the hope that survival is possible; somehow they are discovering how to provide lunches for their children at school and dental care for the family when needed. Take heart from the fact you are not alone: One out of every three children growing up in the United States is currently in a stepfamily.

Let Dallas and Ricki's history bring you some comfort and inspiration. Remarried after each had experienced divorce, they brought a total of five children into a new family unit heavily burdened by money woes.

"By a miracle of God, we were able to buy a house," Ricki says. "It was a stretch for us, especially considering the obligations we already had. We weren't sure how a bank would feel about lending money to a remarried couple. As it turns out, the bank was used to it—they told us it was a common experience.

"We bought a house, struggled to make the payments for the first two years, then discovered our equity had grown high enough to pay off all our other obligations. We took out a home-equity credit line and paid off everything. In another few years, the house had gone up even more in value. We didn't borrow any more money against it, but we sure enjoyed knowing that our net worth had gone up. It changed how we felt about ourselves, not just financially but in other ways too.

"We went from feeling like failures to feeling maybe a little successful. We went from the broken wreckage of the American dream to really living it."

THE FUNCTION OF HOPE IS first of all to change your perception and feelings, then later to begin transforming reality in positive ways. Be frank about your financial situation, but don't stop there. Face your challenges with an accurate realism—but also with unfailing hope. Let optimism and faith carry you forward into a time when life is simpler, money woes are fewer, and your family has what it needs for a good and healthy life.

CHAPTER TWELVE

Break Out the Crazy Glue

Strategies for Sticking Together as a Couple

*In my wildest nightmares, I never saw myself
ending up divorced. In my happiest daydreams,
I could never have imagined how strong, how powerful,
and how loving my second marriage would become.*

FAITH,
17 years into her second marriage

SHEILA LIVES IN THE INNER CITY. At age 38, she's a grand-mother—twice. Were it not for at least five abortions she knows of among her three daughters, she'd be many times more a grandmother. She has mixed feelings about the abortions, but she didn't think her daughters were ready for the burdens of parenthood.

She has married twice and divorced twice. Her current male friend has been part of her life for nearly three years—she lives in his home. However, she is not seriously considering getting married to him.

"He's still too immature," she says. "I might be willing to marry him someday, but not now. He has a lot of growing up to do."

Talking about her own life—not trying to describe a trend—Sheila says softly, "Let's face it, guys come and go. But your kids are your kids forever." She glances at a granddaughter playing nearby. "And so are your grandkids."

Sheila's personal history is not unusual in the early years of the twenty-first century. A broken marriage is no longer rare or remarkable in the civilized nations of the Western world; it's a frequent occurrence and an accepted fact of contemporary life.

More and more typically, younger adults are choosing to live together without marriage, having lost faith in the ability of people, including themselves, to make and keep commitments for a lifetime. Why formalize an arrangement that is viewed as temporary at best? Many believe it's better to leave vows unsaid than to make them and break them. Many who believe this are themselves the children of divorce and broken homes.

As the culture's perception of marriage has weakened, its perception of parenting has correspondingly strengthened. Today's parents, who may have experienced the breakup of numerous pairings as well as several marriages, are increasingly focused on providing a good life for their children. The result is a powerful shift in the overall framework of where adults place their commitments and how they prioritize them.

The First Loyalty Is to the Children

Margie, 26, is technically still married to her second husband. She's in a divorce-recovery group while waiting for the paperwork to work its way through the legal process. She finds needed emotional support and a lot of close friendships among her peers in the divorce-recovery circle.

"We're all in similar situations," she says about the group. "Most of us are in our 20s or 30s, and a lot of us have been married more than once, which really surprised me.

"The one thing we have in common—well, almost all of us—is that we're totally about our children. We live to take care of our kids, to give them the best life possible, to make things easy for them any way we can. Most of our questions in group time are about parenting issues. Most of our discussions, except when the leader is being really structured, are about how to handle the kids, how to solve the problems of being a mom or a dad."

Unknowingly, Margie echoes comments made by Sheila. "I don't know if I'll get married again or not," she sighs. "I'm kind of burned out on marriage right now, to tell you the truth. But what I do know is this—I'm always going to be the mom of my two little guys. And I'm going to be the best mom I know how to be! That's why I'm here in the group."

Without realizing it, Margie and Sheila have each experienced a profound shift in the basis and location of their personal security. Where once a woman might have found her security in the nearby presence of a committed life partner, a modern woman quickly learns that, as Sheila observes, "guys come and go."

This discovery is not a function of gender. Where once a man might have found security in the presence of a lifelong wife for himself and mother for his children, today's man soon learns that at any moment his wife might leave him. The perception of marriage as permanent has been shattered; in its wake, strong feelings of insecurity and uncertainty cause disorder in our private worlds. In the absence of such security we cling to any semblance of permanence that we can find. If we are parents, there is a marked tendency to transfer our need for stability to our role as providers for our sons and daughters.

The New Loyalty Is All About the Children

"I really screwed up our marriage," Daniel says in the aftermath of a messy divorce. "But I'm going to be the best father I can possibly be for my three kids. I know what it's like to grow up as a child of divorce—my dad left us when I was 11. There's no way I'm ever going to leave these kids!"

Is he planning to remarry someday?

"I don't know." He grimaces. "It's not too high on my list

right now. Maybe after the kids are in college. Then again, maybe not. I don't think I could possibly afford two divorces!"

Sheila, Margie, and Daniel do not know each other, yet each has a remarkably similar approach to the future. Remarriage is something that is a possibility, but not being actively pursued. Meanwhile, each of these three adults is passionately trying to be a really good parent for his or her children.

Sheila, not yet 40, is already a grandmother. She has arranged her job so she works second shift, enabling her to be at home during the day to provide child care for one of her grandchildren who is not yet of school age.

"She'll be in pre-K next year," Sheila says of her granddaughter. "And I'm really going to miss my days with her. I feel young again when I'm around her. If I take her to Wal-Mart or to the grocery store, people always think she's my kid! Nobody believes I'm really her grandma."

Margie pays her sister, a single in her early 20s, to watch the kids while Margie is at work. "I'm so glad their aunt is part of their lives," she says of this arrangement. "I want them to grow up knowing all about their family."

For children of divorce, who have experienced the shattering of their home and family life, the passionate attachment of a parent is a powerful positive in a universe of numerous negative feelings and events. Yet if such children are going to develop a balanced and healthy view of what family means, they will need not only the passionate love of their parents, but a living example of parents who are passionately in love with, and permanently committed to, each other.

Adding a New Loyalty Without Abandoning Anyone

One of the great challenges of a remarriage, or even of the serious dating period that generally precedes it, is to transfer loyalty to a new adult without seeming to abandon the level of commitment the children receive.

Some psychologists argue that unless the new marriage is given a place of prominence and importance over and above the parental role, the new household will not be established on a wise foundation. This perspective takes a high view of marriage and focuses on the need of the adults to enter a lasting covenant or a permanent bond that is witnessed by all, including the children.

This perspective, however, ignores the reality that the role of parent has chronologically preceded the remarriage and has thus already achieved a place of prominence and importance higher than the remarriage, at least in the beginning. Denying the importance of this history may not be advisable. Some argue it's not even a realistic possibility. "Your kids are your kids forever," as Sheila observes.

Advocating the permanence of a remarriage need not demote the children to a lesser role, regardless of the theoretical value of such a demotion. Rather, the task of the remarried parent is to attach a strong loyalty to the new partner while not in any way disconnecting the strong loyalty already bestowed on the children.

Paulette found herself surprised by her eight-year-old. "Mommy, do you love Tom (the new husband) more than you love me?" asked her daughter. The late-night question came with a level of emotional intensity that betrayed the fear and uncertainty Paulette's daughter was feeling just a few weeks after the remarriage.

Paulette had not anticipated the question. "I didn't know what to say," she remembers. "But I knew I'd better have a pretty good answer. So I breathed a silent prayer asking God for wisdom, and I just took my daughter's hand in mine, and looked at her. In that instant, somehow I knew what to say.

"I can't imagine loving anyone more than I love you," Paulette told her daughter that evening at bedtime. "I don't think it's possible. I love you so much! But if you're asking me whether I love Tom a lot, I want you to know something. I really do love him! And I hope when you grow up, you'll love him, too."

By divine grace or through human wisdom, Paulette's answer illustrates an approach that may prove helpful for parents that remarry. By every possible method, continue to reassure your children of your enduring love. Be certain you are just as loving, just as caring, just as fully present with your children as you were before the new adult relationship entered your life. In this way, you make it clear the children are not "losing" anything—which is their fear.

At the same time, if the remarriage is going to achieve its purposes of becoming a lifelong relationship, changing the way in which your children may view marriage and family life, the new adult must sooner or later receive the same level of loyalty the children already receive. Nothing less will suffice.

"MY CHILDREN HADN'T LOST their mom," Ron comments. "She lived nearby and we shared custody, so they had access to their mother all the time. They never lost that important connection to their birth mother, and I was glad. However, I felt kind of awkward when I brought Sandi into my life. Without realizing I was doing it, I tried to hide my love for Sandi when the kids were around. It was like I was ashamed of loving Sandi, or maybe I was afraid to show how much I really loved her.

"It was really awkward when I had the kids and Sandi was with us. Sandi noticed it first—I was changing the way I behaved toward her when the kids were around us in our home."

How did Ron deal with the problem once he realized it?

"Sandi just told me to be myself. She said the kids were old enough to handle the fact I loved her a lot. She even said the kids would be happy I loved her a lot—they'd enjoy seeing our love."

Did it work out that way?

"Actually, I still felt awkward for a long time," Ron admits.

"But I did try to be more open and natural about my love for Sandi with the kids around. And over time, it got to where I was treating Sandi the same way when the kids were with us as I did when the kids were at their mother's."

What was the outcome of this transition?

"My daughter was the first to make a comment. She was the one I kind of worried about. She was the only female, and she had been really close to her mom when she was younger, so I worried about how she would feel when I brought another woman into my life.

"One night after I'd gotten more relaxed about letting the kids see how much I loved Sandi, my daughter caught up with me in the kitchen. For a minute only the two of us were in there. She said, 'You really love Sandi, don't you?' and I admitted that I loved Sandi immensely. Then she said, 'I can tell that Sandi is really good for you. I'm glad she's in your life right now'—and I almost lost it! I seriously almost cried on the spot, and I'm not a crier," Ron claims. "It meant so much that my daughter not only saw my love for Sandi, but also approved of it and supported it."

Ron had managed the difficult task of maintaining a strong commitment to his children while also establishing a strong, permanent bond with a new partner. He hadn't read any books on the topic; he was finding his way by trial and error.

Today, nearly ten years after his remarriage, Ron's primary task as a parent is nearly complete. His youngest child will soon leave home. Meanwhile, his role as Sandi's husband appears to have many decades ahead of it, all of which causes him great satisfaction.

"I'm going to be with Sandi forever," he announces. "So I'm glad I learned how to admit my love for her when the kids were around. I wonder what might have happened if Sandi hadn't been so wise. I sometimes wonder what would have happened if I would have let my fear of being open cause me to lose Sandi completely!"

"It wouldn't have happened." Sandi interrupts for the first time. "I had signed up for the 'life' plan." She takes her husband's hand in hers, and the two of them seem like partners of 20 or 30 years, rather than nearly 10.

SHOULD THE NEW PARTNER BE more important in your life than the children? Should the children be more important in your life than the new partner? The experts submit varying opinions on the question.

While they continue their debate, remarried partners are finding that the best approach may be to keep on loving the children as you always have while also making it clear that the new adult in the home is deeply loved. Just as it is possible to be permanently and forever loyal to more than one child, so also it is possible to be lastingly loyal to a new partner as well as to all your children.

Ron and Sandi are living proof, as are many others.

Carve Out "Family Time" to Reinforce Your Loyalty

One way to let children know your love is enduring is to create times of special meaning for them. Although your task as a parent means that you are constantly busy caring for your children, your children may not notice! Yet they will definitely notice when you establish special times to celebrate being together as a family. Their memory banks will retain the significance of these times.

Barb and Larry take their kids, her two and his one, to pizza and a movie every Friday night. "We go during the afternoon matinee price," Barb points out, "so it's not horribly expensive."

The three children, all of whom are of elementary-school age, obviously look forward to Friday nights. On Thursday, when the movie theater releases its new schedule of showings, the family sits down during dinner and chooses the film that will be seen the next night.

"It's a weekly tradition for us," Larry says. "And between the pizza and the popcorn and the movies, it's not cheap. But we wanted to send a message to the kids that we love them, and that this family is going to stay together. Probably when the kids are older we won't be able to do this all the time, but we're going to keep doing it as long as we possibly can!"

Barb concurs. "I wasn't able to spend money like this when I was alone. My kids mattered to me, but I couldn't afford to take them out for pizza once a week, let alone take them out for *both* pizza *and* a movie every Friday.

"Sometimes I worry about what it's costing us, but mostly I'm just thankful we can afford it so far," she continues. "All three of our kids look forward to Friday nights. It's their favorite time of the week, and no wonder!"

Barb and Larry's intention was to give the new family a chance to bond together and become a unified group. Thus far, the strategy seems to be working. Yet a secondary benefit is to send a message to the children that they are highly important and valued members of the new household. As they grow and mature, they'll eventually realize mom and dad are making financial sacrifices to provide the weekly entertainment for the household.

"They know we love them," Larry declares. "And hopefully they know that from our words and our actions, not just from pizza and movies. But sometimes kids realize things when they're done in a tangible way. When we spend our whole Friday night with the family every Friday night, that shows the kids that they're important to us, they're a huge priority in our lives!"

Since remarriage introduces an element of change and uncertainty into the lives of children, it can be extremely meaningful to counteract that uncertainty by building intentional family time, with the children as a focus, into the new life and rituals of the remarriage family.

Children are reassured by the presence of these new rituals, and their fears are assuaged by the evident love from both partners. Establishing the children and their happiness as a priority in the new relationship is a healthy way of sending children the message that they are valued, cared about, and respected.

Carve Out "Couple Time" Without Feeling Guilty

When the children are being treated as a priority and their level of importance is clearly established by family rituals and practices, there is more than enough room to also establish the new couple relationship as a high value.

If remarried couples err in setting their priorities, it is often at this point. Afraid of alienating the children, worried perhaps about losing their affection, new mates may indefinitely postpone their own times of bonding, romance, and special occasions. As the evidence indicates, they do so at their own peril. Without access to privacy, intimacy, and romantic interludes, the new relationship may perish before it ever strikes down roots. Its collapse may even seem to be welcomed by the children—who may have viewed it as a threat—but in the long term, yet another model of breakdown in front of the children is neither healthy nor wise.

Besides needing to have certainty they are loved and valued, children need the comfort of knowing the adults in their home are in love and at peace. Children of divorce know all too well about the warning signs of a decline. Raised voices, frequent arguments, times of abandonment or silence—children will read these signals and know what they mean. Their fears will surface early and intensify quickly.

Remarried parents need not feel guilty about using time, space, and finances to make their new union a priority. A helpful way of viewing your "couple time" is to see it as the best kind of role-modeling for your children—showing them two adults in love with each other who clearly feel romantic about each other, and who are obviously growing closer together as time passes.

One benefit that accrues from the liability of a past divorce is that custody of the children may be shared with someone else. If this is true, the possibility of "child-free" weekends or holidays becomes very real, which permits a couple to establish time for each other in a way that does not diminish family time.

"Both of us had kids," Gary says of his remarriage. "And both of us had ex's who lived nearby and shared custody. So we got this brainstorm one day—that maybe we could manage to farm out the kids at the same time, at least sometimes.

"Like everything else, this bright idea didn't always work. A lot of times we thought we had the custody times lined up at the same time, but then something would change. We'd end up having one set of kids with us while the other set was gone to the other parent.

"That worked too, actually, because it gave us time as a couple with just one set of kids—so that was okay," he continues. "But the really great times were when we got both custodies to line up, both of our ex's had the kids at the same time, and we were just totally free as a couple!

"Does that sound selfish? Sorry! But those times were great! And even though it often fell through, it worked out enough that we got some really great couple time in ways that were kind of invisible to the kids."

Not every remarried couple brings two sets of children into the new union. Obviously, if only one partner has children with shared custody, it may be simpler to achieve couple time when the kids are with the other parent.

"We go to Palm Springs," says one Southern California couple. "We take the kids to their mom's house on Friday (for weekend visits) and then we just keep driving. We can be in Palm Springs before sunset, and we usually stay there until Sunday afternoon. It's become our own little getaway time!"

Such indulgences are beyond the budget of many remarried families, yet good couple time does not require a hotel suite in a desert oasis.

"Our house is empty every other weekend," Melinda says, smiling. "The kids go to visit their dad, and that leaves Phil and me alone at home. We sometimes don't even leave the house," she says, blushing. "We always talk about all the things we're going to do while the kids are gone, but sometimes it's just more relaxing to stay home and do nothing."

Melinda has heard of the "date night" concept many marriage counselors recommend for married and remarried couples. "(We) can't afford it," she says. "Who has the money to go out to dinner every week? We don't! But luckily the kids' dad takes them every other weekend. He's been pretty reliable, especially now that he got married to Debbie. So we can plan on having every other weekend all to ourselves. Those weekends have become some of the best times of our married life…"

Instead of always viewing shared custody as an obstacle or hassle, try viewing it as a liberating factor for finding quality couple time. It may change your entire perception of shared custody.

Show Your Children This Marriage Is Forever

In our work with children of divorce—now spanning nearly three decades—we deal with the recurring hope of such children that their mother and father will one day be remarried—to each other. This dream is powerful and pervasive, as well as natural and normal and commendable. We do not discourage it; we often wish we could somehow make it come true.

Reality is more complicated. Many divorced persons remarry and establish new households and new families. Not uncommonly, both parents remarry after a divorce, and both parents establish new family circles. Thus in order for the dream of the original family's children to come true, two new families would have to be shattered, two new sets of vows broken and lost.

Is this what we should wish for? In our attempt to rebuild what once was, should we destroy all that is? Or is it more healthy to begin where we are and attempt to build new models of successful and thriving marriages for our children to witness? How does it seem to you?

Ministers and theologians vary in their responses to this question. Some wish to avoid the fact of remarriage altogether, insisting it shouldn't occur. This conveniently ignores the real lives of a greatly increasing number of American families.

Theology is often more tidy than life. Living is complicated, and for those involved in the aftermath of divorce and the existence of multiple remarriages, reality is a daily struggle to balance priorities and raise healthy children.

The stories, experiences, strategies, values, and perspectives we have put down in this book aim at one purpose: to transform the marriage in which you now are into a union that will endure for life, ending only when "death do us part," as the traditional vow proclaims.

Is this a false hope, an impossible dream, a ridiculous goal? Day after day, the real lives of remarried couples and families say "no" to this question. Difficult as it is, these people are finding the tools they need to begin where they are, face life as it is, and build a lifelong marriage relationship.

Many are discovering help within their communities of faith, finding they are surrounded in the pews by other remarried persons, who face similar challenges. Whether or not theology and preaching eventually catch up with reality, the pioneers of enduring remarriages are busy making and keeping commitments to God, each other, and their children.

ON OUR DRIVE TO ATTEND the fiftieth wedding anniversary of a remarried couple, we reflected on this new framework for success. Not ever knowing the original partnerships the husband

and wife were in, we were sad that any marriage, at any time, had ended. (It is our hope and prayer that every marriage, every time, be forever.) Yet somehow sadness was not our main emotion as we drove across the beautiful wooded hills of Wisconsin to attend the celebration. Yes, there was brokenness in the past. But there was also something else—something wonderful and good and very much worth celebrating.

For 50 years, this partnership formed by remarriage had modeled godly living and loving parenthood. For half a century, this couple who had promised to love, honor, and cherish each other had done exactly that. It had been our privilege to know them for nearly two decades of that time, and to know their children and grandchildren also.

Knowing how few original marriages reach the 50-year mark, we were elated and deeply touched that a remarriage had gone this distance. Unknown to us then, the remarriage would last another half-dozen years before death parted it.

We drank coffee, we ate cake, we looked at photographs. We listened to stories, and we took some pictures of our own. We laughed with a large and loving family, and we felt included among it as if we were related.

We had a party—one of the best parties ever.

May it be so for you, too.

One day in the future, may there be a 10-year anniversary party, or a 25-year anniversary party. If you are young enough today, may there be a 50-year anniversary party for your remarriage. (Invite us, and we'll try to be there!)

Imagine yourself at that party as a guest of honor, showing friends and neighbors and relatives the photo albums of your long and successful union. Imagine your children and grandchildren attending; imagine them speaking at your party and talking about the great example set by your marriage.

Imagine it, dream it, and pray it, because by the grace of God, it is a very real possibility for you. Amid the wreckage of past dreams—and in the midst of a culture that devalues commitment, you are able by God's grace to "go the distance" and become a new kind of role model for everyone around you.

It may not be easy, yet nothing valuable ever is.

IN SOME QUAKER WEDDINGS, there is a ceremony called "the bitter and the sweet." The minister shares with the bridal couple that life will bring them both kinds of experiences, the bitter and the sweet. One of the couple's first acts together is to sip first vinegar, then honey from two cups, realizing that life is a mixed blessing—a complex experience involving both suffering and celebration.

The ceremony points us to a great truth about ourselves and our lives. If you have experienced the brokenness of divorce and the end of a previous marriage, you may have already tasted from the "bitter" chalice. Whether or not you choose to remarry, our prayer for you is that life brings you other types of experiences also, memories that are sweet and good and healing.

If you have chosen to remarry and are busy raising a family in this kind of relationship, our prayer for you is that this new union will bring you much more honey than vinegar—and that much more of what is true and good will surround you and fill you in this new family setting.

May you find the courage to hope, and may your hopes be exceeded by the good things God unfolds for you within the new union. At the party where you celebrate the anniversary of a lengthy relationship, may you be surrounded by those you love, and may they affirm and praise you for being a great example in marriage.

By the grace of God, may this reality be your future.

The Story
You Live In

❀

$\mathcal{A}$s a reader of this book, you may be a remarried person or someone who lives in a blended family. About 90 million people in the United States are now living in a stepfamily, and the number is growing daily.

As we travel the United States, Canada, and other nations, we continue to meet courageous, hope-filled people who have survived divorce. Many of these have found the grace of a positive and happy remarriage—now they're doing the best they can to raise their children in a loving, supportive family environment.

Life is difficult for these men and women. They're coping with their own personal pain as they make every effort to help their children adjust, adapt, and thrive. It's often hard to allow time for your own healing when your first priority is to care for your children, your new partner, and everyone else around you.

Are we describing your life and your story?

Our hope in writing this book was to suggest some pathways that might ease your journey, allowing you to learn from the experiences of others who are also struggling to form healthy, well-adjusted families. If you've found in these few pages some strategies that are clear, workable, and practical, then maybe God has helped you find these stories for your sake and the sake of those you love.

Meanwhile, your own story continues. How is the story you find yourself in?

"I keep waiting for the 'and they lived happily ever after' part," one busy wife and mother shared with us recently. "It seems like every time Don and I solve one of our problems, two more problems pop up and surprise us!"

Welcome to life in a remarriage: It's about constantly learning and growing and facing new challenges. Yet like all learning and growing, the seasons do change—not every experience is a trauma, not every problem is a crisis. Sometimes when you least expect it, grace happens.

WE CONTINUE TO MEET HAPPY, well-adjusted people who are making their remarriages healthy and hope-filled. None of them have found it easy, and most of them confess they have often thought of giving up, especially early in the new relationship. But they have one thing in common. They're glad they didn't quit when things got tough, because now—finally—things are getting better.

Can you imagine your story getting better?

God can.

In writing this book we have tried not to minimize the challenges you are facing. Your challenges are serious, complex, and tenacious—as you begin to learn how to address one issue, other issues seem to emerge. You feel like a boxer in the late rounds, taking blows from every side, just trying to stay on your feet until the bell rings so you can get some rest!

God knows all about that.

If you've been abandoned by a partner, if you've watched a

marriage end, if there are dark chapters in the story of your life—God knows.

Somewhere in the midst of your darkness, a tiny light is glowing—maybe just a candle in the wind, but the light is there. The purpose of that light is to draw you onward toward safer places, times of healing, seasons of hope. Writing to the church at Rome, the apostle Paul put it this way: "We know that in all things God works for good with those who love him" (Romans 8:28).

In all things? In things like being abandoned, being sued for divorce, being left alone to raise your kids with no money and no help? In things like this?

In all things.

In things like finding a new partner, forming a new family, showing your children a different kind of example of being married.

In things like learning how to admit your anger instead of hiding it, finding ways to solve your arguments without yelling so loudly, fitting the children of someone else into the family you already have.

In all things.

Paul's reminder is something we need to keep in front of us...maybe stuck to the refrigerator with a magnet or taped to the dashboard of the minivan. "God is at work for good—in all things" is something we need to remember.

Let God invade your story with His grace.

Let His forgiveness begin to cover all the places where you hurt, where you are angry—even the places where you've made mistakes of your own. Let God's good ideas begin to replace the hopelessness you so often feel.

Your story matters, and perhaps this book is one of the candles or lights God will use to move your story forward in His good ways.

Keep moving toward the light, even when you feel you can't go on.

Keep believing that the days ahead can be brighter and better, even if your progress seems so very slow at times.

Keep forgiving everyone around you—they need it—but save a little of that forgiveness for yourself. You may be imperfect and flawed, and you may have made some spectacular mistakes in your life, but if so, that only proves one thing—you are human like all the rest of us.

Be open to God's little surprises, like when hope springs up after one of your worst moments. Turn away from the darkness and face that tiny candle, away off in the distance. Move in that direction, even if you have to crawl.

Somewhere in the future—or perhaps even now—may the story of your life encounter the light of God's good hope, surrounding you with the forgiveness and faith that make all things new.

—David and Lisa
June 2005

Questions for
Discussion and Thought

✿

$\mathcal{A}$S WE TRAVEL TO SPEAK AT RETREATS AND SEMINARS, God continues to bring us high-intensity and high-quality interaction with remarried couples. Their stories fill the pages of this book, and as you might expect—there are many valuable and interesting stories that simply wouldn't fit within these pages. If you are somewhere along the remarriage journey, we'd love to know about your story also!*

MEANWHILE, WE'VE WRITTEN THE QUESTIONS in this next section to help you interact with the primary concepts of this book. Answering these questions, thinking them over, and discussing them as a couple may prove helpful in moving your remarriage relationship in positive directions. If you'd like to note your answers on the pages, we've provided space for you to do so.

---

* The best way to share your story with us would be to send it to any of the e-mail addresses on our Web site: www.MarriageStudies.com. (See "About the Authors" at the back of this book for more contact information.) Although we do not provide online marriage counseling, we'll definitely send you a note letting you know we received your story. If we consider your story for a future book project, we'll contact you (please provide your contact information) to discuss that.

DISCUSSION GUIDE
CHAPTER ONE

The Journey Begins

WE OPENED THIS BOOK with the story of Mark and Joanie getting remarried at the Mall of America in Bloomington, Minnesota. Their wedding ceremony included the children each of them were bringing into the new union. Their wedding service was brief, positive, and friendly—and their guest list was small.

Here are some questions that story brings up:

1. How does this story remind you of your own remarriage ceremony? Did you choose an elaborate wedding with many attendants and guests? Did both partners have family members and relatives present at the wedding service? Were your children, your partner's children, or both involved in the wedding ceremony itself?

2. On the day of your remarriage, what were your primary emotions? Were you excited about returning to married life? Were you nervous about the "odds for success" of this new union? Would you describe your emotions that day as joyous, celebrative, and relaxed—or would you use words like *anxious, nervous,* and *tentative?*

3. Thinking about the remarriage ceremony, were both you and your partner actively involved in the planning of the service? Were you married by clergy? What are some of your most positive memories from the service, reception, and wedding day?

4. How much premarriage counseling did you receive? How does this compare with the amount of counseling you received before your previous marriage?

5. If you received premarriage counseling, how helpful was it? Did your counselor or minister seem to understand the unique issues and pressures involved in a remarriage? Did you feel free to express your true feelings in the counseling situation? If so, did you go ahead and express those feelings?

6. If you could speak directly to remarriage couples *before* they got remarried, what would you say to them about premarital counseling? What would you advise them about planning the wedding ceremony? What other advice would you give?

7. If you could go back and restart your own remarriage, what is the one thing you would most likely try to "do over" and change for the better? What changes would you make in the way that you and your partner started out on your new journey?

DISCUSSION GUIDE
CHAPTER TWO

Form a Spiritual Connection Centered on Serving God

1. What's *your* answer to this question we've asked other remarried couples: Thinking about your previous experience of marriage, would you say that both partners, only one of you, or neither of you were serious about God?

2. Do you consider your spiritual life a "separate" category, unrelated to things like your physical health, emotional stability, and marital satisfaction? Did reading this chapter cause you to consider

that these issues—health, happiness, attitude, spirituality—may all be interrelated and connected somehow?

3. Have you and your spouse made a serious and sustained effort to pray together? Did you find it difficult to get started? Would you consider a "trial period"—of one week, one month, or some other length of time—during which you would try praying together? Might your relationship change for the better if the two of you were united in prayer?

4. Are you and your partner involved—together—in a growth group or small group sponsored by your faith community? Do you have access to joining such a group? Have you been asked to lead a group of this type? Does your church or congregation offer a group that is specifically for remarried couples?

5. Does your denomination or local church offer "missions trip" possibilities for you to consider? What have you heard about Habitat for Humanity? How might it change your marriage relationship if you and your partner worked together—side by side—doing something good for someone else, either overseas or right in your own community?

6. Do you and your partner attend worship together? Are you able to experience the same service together at the same time, or is one of you (or both) busy helping in another area or another ministry during the worship service? Can you adjust your schedules so that both of you can share in worship together, side by side?

7. Do you have a "spiritual leader" in your own home? If so, which of you fills that role or function? Would you say that you are

growing spiritually as a couple? Are both of you making progress in overcoming old negative patterns and building positive new habits? Is spiritual growth—personally and as a married couple—a high priority for you?

DISCUSSION GUIDE
CHAPTER THREE

Regard Your Remarriage as Permanent and Irreversible

1. Are you living in a cardboard box while reading these words? (If not, thank God!) Are you regarding your remarriage as "temporary shelter"—or as permanent housing? Have you started to think about your remarriage in terms of forever?

2. Have you already experienced "tough times" or "great difficulties" within your remarried life? If so, did you approach those realities with fear—afraid that the remarriage might end? Or with confidence—deciding to stay together no matter what?

3. What is happening within your remarriage that makes you feel successful? Can you identify areas within your remarried family life that seem to be working? Make a list of things that you are doing "right" as a couple or family. Take your time, think carefully about your marriage and family life—and find some successes to celebrate!

4. If there are children living in your home, what kind of example are you showing them about married life, romantic love between

a couple, and lasting commitment? Would you say that the children in your home (his, hers, ours) are seeing a different kind of example than they may have seen previously? If so, is the new example more positive?

5. When children sense commitment, endurance, and permanence in the lives of their custodial parents, they tend to feel safer. They tend to do better in school, improve their behavior in social settings, and generally relax into new routines and realities. Have you seen any of these positive changes in your children? Are you sending them the message that your remarriage is headed for "forever"? Have you told them so verbally?

6. How does the remarriage story of Ronald and Nancy Reagan make you feel? Did you realize that their much-publicized romantic love was part of a second marriage? Can you see how, regardless of past experience with marriage, it is more than possible for a person to find a committed, lasting, romantic union?

7. How does the story of Fred and Verna Beffa make you feel? With 56 years of happy remarriage, they are the current "record holders" among remarried couples we have personally known. How would you like to challenge their record and become the next champions in this category? How many years have you been remarried?

DISCUSSION GUIDE
CHAPTER FOUR

Forgive Everyone, Including Yourself

1. In your own spiritual journey, have you found forgiveness from God for the faults, failures, and sins that are part of your

own spiritual baggage? Are you living in God's light as a forgiven person, confident and certain that God forgives and welcomes you? If you have not done so recently, read and contemplate John 3:17.

2. In thinking about your previous experience with marriage, are there ways in which you need to be forgiven for your own behaviors and choices? Should you consider asking for forgiveness from your children, your former spouse, or other persons? Have you talked about these issues with a clergyperson, counselor, or trusted friend?

3. In thinking about your previous experience with marriage, are there persons that have hurt or harmed you? Have you spent time waiting for these persons to come and ask you to forgive them? Are you still waiting? After reading this chapter, are you beginning to understand the value of forgiving these people—even if they never ask you to forgive them—even though they may not deserve your gracious forgiveness? Do you realize that none of us, not one, deserves our forgiveness from God?

4. In what ways are you holding on to anger, hurt feelings, or a sense of injustice based on things that have happened in the past? After reading this chapter, are you beginning to understand that health and healing can replace the inner tension you've been feeling? Do you understand that positive physical and emotional changes can occur as you release and relinquish these feelings of anger, hostility, resentment, and bitterness?

5. Are you making forgiveness a "core value" in your remarriage relationship? Are you making a conscious choice to forgive your current partner for his or her oversights, faults, and mistakes? Do you realize you have married a human being, and that all of us— all human—are going to keep making mistakes and keep having some faults? Do you understand how helpful it is to forgive your partner as you build your remarriage?

6. In what ways do you sometimes feel like "damaged goods" or a "broken person"? Have you talked with a minister, a counselor, or a trusted friend about these feelings? After reading this chapter, are you beginning to understand the value and importance of forgiving yourself? In trying to do so, do you think it would be helpful to have a trained therapist, a close friend, a minister, or your spouse at your side, helping you do this difficult work?

DISCUSSION GUIDE
CHAPTER FIVE

Use Conflict to Get Better Acquainted

1. How did your remarriage relationship begin? Did the relationship start as a friendship and become "romantic" at a later time? At what point did you first notice conflict as a part of the relationship? Did conflict arise before you remarried? How did you tend to resolve your differences before becoming husband and wife?

2. One of the couples in this chapter seemed to be "conflict-free" in the first seasons of their remarried life. Why did it seem this way? Is your relationship similar in any way to the relationship of this particular couple? Is your relationship seemingly "conflict-free" because one of you, or both, are withholding your true opinions and identity?

3. Do you understand and agree with the concept of "not while you're hot" in dealing with conflict? Are you able, even when angry and upset, to wait and talk about the issue at a later time—when your emotions are under control? Are both partners able to keep a lid on their emotions and feelings, and behave appropriately when angry? Did you grasp and agree with the idea that anger itself is not wrong, but clinging to it is unhelpful?

4. Have you tried the method of waiting to resolve an argument or disagreement until *both of you* are ready to talk? In general, does one of you tend to avoid talking about issues? In general, does one of you tend to "pressure" or "push" the other into having discussions and resolving areas of conflict or difficulty?

5. Can you relate to Chaz and Karen's conflict while driving? Did you understand the focus of that particular section—that is, to express your feelings without making an attack on the character, worth, dignity, or skill of your partner? How often do you make a careless remark that denigrates or "cuts down" your partner's self-esteem or self-worth? Learning to change your style of communication can be hugely helpful for both of you.

6. Have you noticed whether you tend to become defensive when someone questions you? Have you ever overreacted to a simple, well-meaning question because you felt like you were being attacked in some way? Work on beginning to notice your emotions, particularly during times of discussion or argument. Focus on how you *feel* when your partner asks a question or makes a statement.

When you do this, do you sometimes find yourself feeling flustered, upset, or angry? Do you think it's because you may be starting to get defensive? Learning to express your feelings without "defending" yourself can help keep arguments from escalating and careening out of control.

7. Who is the most outgoing and verbal, you or your partner? In social settings, does one of you tend to remain silent while the other one speaks? In private conversation, is there a similar pattern—one of you doing all the talking while the other listens?

Having different personalities and different levels of verbal communication is completely fine. However, if one of you is particularly verbal, that one needs to learn how to listen more. Listening precedes learning!

And if one of you is often silent, try speaking up and speaking out. You need not start an argument or raise an objection—just try offering your opinion. Your partner may learn some needed and helpful things if you'll just speak up!

8. Have you ever explained something to your partner, only to discover that he or she wasn't really listening? Perhaps you were talking at the wrong moment—while your partner was reading, watching TV, or thinking intently about something else.

Being an attentive spouse means focusing your interest when your partner is speaking to you. Try to stop what you're doing and listen well. As you listen, give your partner both verbal and nonverbal feedback that shows you are paying attention.

As you listen, ask questions that interact with the subject. In this way, you can begin to have a conversation, rather than merely a speech. In this way, a "monologue" can become a "dialogue," and better learning can occur.

Your First Choices

1. Are you considering having a "big wedding" the second time around? What do you think about your plans after going through the chart below?

Some of the advantages	Some of the challenges
Publicly seeking God's blessing on your new union	Lack of finances
Creating positive memories for your children	Possibility of offending relatives and family
Registering for and receiving gifts from friends and family	Seems too soon to be "asking" for gifts again
Beginning your new family with a joyous celebration	Other priorities for your limited resources

2. Are you considering a honeymoon for the two of you? What do you think about your plans after going through the chart below?

Some of the advantages	Some of the challenges
Getting away from the stresses of your recent life	Stretching resources too thin; creating additional financial stress
Time together as a couple without tasks of parenting	Infants or young children needing parental attention
Never had a honeymoon in the prior marriage(s)	Lack of vacation time from employers of one or both
Beginning your life as a couple with a joyous celebration	Other priorities can't be postponed or avoided

3. Have you thought about having a "familymoon" experience? What do you think about your plans after going through the chart below?

Some of the advantages	Some of the challenges
A fun way to start blending two families into one	Friction among siblings can emerge right from the start
Creating new traditions for your new family	Finding activities and choices that "everyone" seems to enjoy
Beginning new family life in a "neutral zone" away from home	Children are already sensitive to issues of "equal" treatment
Expressing and showing love for each child in your new family	Not enough funds for the whole family to "get away"

Your Place or Mine?

Housing Questions for Empty-Nesters

1. Even if your children aren't living under your roof, how important is it that you live in close proximity to them?

2. If shared or occasional custody will be a factor, what transportation issues are related to your choice of housing?

3. Your place or mine—does it make sense for two of you to share a space currently owned or rented by one of you?

4. How do you want to live? In other words, what are some of your core values and favorite shared activities as a couple?

5. Might it be simpler, cheaper, or otherwise an advantage to "start over" in a home that neither of you have lived in?

Housing Questions When Only One of You Has Resident Children

1. How important is it (to the birth parent) that the children remain in their present home, keeping changes at a minimum?

2. How important is it (to the birth parent) that the children remain enrolled in their same schools—or within the boundaries of their current school district? Might change be beneficial?

3. Does the new partner feel uncomfortable about "taking the place" of someone by moving in? Might the children see this new adult as attempting to "replace" their parent?

4. How strong are the advantages—if any—of starting your new life as a family in a location that is brand-new for all of you?

5. How will your family budget be affected by your housing decision?

Housing Questions When Both of You Have Resident Children

1. Do you both realize you are attempting the most difficult of all remarriage/housing scenarios? Are you prepared for conflict?

2. Will any of the children be close in age to a new sibling? Are any of these cases teens, especially teen females? Have you considered potential rivalry and jealousy issues in making room arrangements?

3. Have you met together as an entire new family with a qualified marriage or family counselor to talk about housing-related issues?

4. Have both adults listened carefully to the perspective and feelings of each child? Have the children felt free to express their thoughts?

5. Are all of you (especially adults and teens) prepared to make some difficult compromises so that someone else in the family benefits? Are all of you trying to think "win–win" regarding your housing?

DISCUSSION GUIDE
CHAPTER EIGHT

Who's the Boss?

1. As you thought about getting remarried, were you secretly (or openly) hoping to gain a new disciplinarian around the house? Did you hope that bringing a new "mom" or "dad" into the home would teach your children how to behave themselves properly? What does this chapter suggest to you about the dangers of this approach? Whose job is it (first and foremost) to shape, mold, guide and direct your children?

2. What do you think of the recommendation by remarried families—as well as marriage and family therapists—of "letting the birth parent be the boss parent"? Does this make sense to you now that you've read this chapter? How might your children reject an "outside" authority or resent your new partner for trying to control them? Can you see how beneficial it is for your new partner to come into the household without assuming that kind of a burden or difficulty?

3. Do you personally have parents, siblings, or friends who reinforce your role as the parent of your children, helping you establish boundaries and monitor behaviors? How might your new partner might serve a similar role—"watching your back" as you carry out your parental duties? If you are the new partner, how can you avoid undermining the authority of the birth parent or

establishing different rules and boundaries instead of reinforcing the existing ones?

4. Are you willing to wait to be liked until later? Are you willing to be "tough" and "firm" in the early days of your remarriage, backing up the birth parent's rules and practices, even if the children seem angry with you? Are you prepared to be tested, and tested again, by your new partner's children? How, specifically, do you think these issues might come up in your new family?

It's natural to want your new partner's children to accept you and like you. However, it's far more important that they respect you—especially while setting up the household. Although everyone likes to be liked, make it your aim to be respected. Treat everyone fairly but firmly, without trying to "bribe" your way into a child's affection.

5. If you and your partner both have children at home, are you content to let each other keep on disciplining your own children in your own ways? Can you live with the fact that there may be two sets of discipline in the house, since there are also two sets of kids? Are you willing to learn from your partner's approach to discipline? How might you do this?

6. Are you prepared for the inevitable whining of young children (or adolescents) if your partner's kids seem to have a better deal than they do, discipline-wise? Can you be patient as you explain— as many times as necessary—that your same boundaries and rules are going to keep on applying, even in the new family? What do you think you might say to them?

DISCUSSION GUIDE
CHAPTER NINE

Blend It Like the Bradys

1. If you're already trying to "blend" two sets of children into one new family, have you found it incredibly difficult? If so, did you think of this as some sort of failure?

Try not to judge yourself by your worst day; instead, aim for small successes along the way, expecting the road to be rough. Is it possible that you're doing something right? Think for a moment about some successes you've had and some good times you've shared already. Celebrate!

2. Have you already found yourself trying to "force" unity, togetherness, and a strong sense of family? How can you "back off" if necessary?

There are no shortcuts to the kind of group unity, family sharing, and positive memories that you hope to build. Keep telling yourself to back off and be patient—good things come if you wait.

3. Have you learned to celebrate what is, rather than pretending all is normal? Think over some ways your new family could do this.

Blended families, perhaps more than other family types, already understand that life involves loss, suffering, and change. As you make your challenging journey toward unity as a new family, take time to stop and celebrate the good things along the way. A new job? Celebrate! Some good grades? Party!

4. Are you brave enough to dare bathrobe caroling? (Note to parents: the concept here is to be fully layered and fully dressed beneath the bathrobes!) What other ideas can you brainstorm for new family traditions?

Building new traditions is one of the "fun parts" of establishing your new family. Okay, maybe your first three ideas (or first eight, or first twenty) won't be runaway successes: just keep trying! (Who knows? Maybe your tradition will be wild and crazy enough to make it into the pages of our next book!)

DISCUSSION GUIDE
CHAPTER TEN

The "X" Factor

JUST A QUICK REMINDER HERE: Did somebody say that divorce and remarriage were going to be *easy?*
You already know better.

1. Your ex-partner may be driving you crazy. But one of you needs to be the grown-up. And since your ex-partner isn't measuring up, that means it's your turn. Can you be patient when your ex-partner tests you, then tests you again? Can you be responsible, even when your ex-partner isn't? What specific choices can you make to act maturely even when your ex-spouse isn't doing so?

2. Can you explain your point of view without attacking or yelling at your "ex"? Can you control your emotions, at least on the outside? What "plans" can you think up to help you prepare to do this better?

Talk to your "ex" with care and restraint. Hint: Your kids are watching you!

3. How do you speak about your ex-partner, especially when the kids are listening? Do you find yourself complaining about his or her behavior, constantly telling your kids about faults, imperfections, and failings? Who can blame you? Yet it's time for a change. List some specific situations where you tend to do this. How can you change your behavior?

Speaking positively about your ex-partner, especially around your kids, sets the kind of example you want your kids to see and hear. You don't have to lie—after all, your "ex" probably isn't perfect. Neither are you. The key is to avoid whittling away at the respect your children *should have* for their birth parent.

4. Are you in a situation where your ex-partner's relatives—perhaps especially the parents—continue to be supportive of the entire family? How is this helpful? How is it difficult? What could you do to improve things?

Even if your ex-relatives aren't particularly warm to you, realize that they still feel connected—and they are—to your children. Try to be as generous and fair-minded as possible. Continue to let your children interact with their grandparents and other relatives from your previous marriage—the continuity will help the children adapt and thrive.

For Poor or Poorer

How much money did Mike Brady make anyway? What a beautiful home, what nice cars and clothes, what a great lifestyle the Bradys had—they even went to Hawaii! The Brady backstory (watch the first episode) involves the death of Mike's wife, not a divorce. So perhaps the secret is that Mike wasn't paying alimony or child-care expenses.

In any case, most remarriages begin with shared financial deficits, not surplus.

1. Have you and your new partner had candid, open, deep discussions about money? Have you told each other the truth about your pre-remarriage financial condition? What do you need to say now, if you haven't said it previously?

If you are considering professional counseling, including financial topics in the counseling is a wise way to proceed. If you don't feel the need for counseling in other areas, simply seeing a professional financial planner may make sense. In any event, can you be open and honest with your partner?

2. In your new family unit, does each of you seem to have very different priorities, especially when it comes to spending money on the children? How do you feel about accepting the differences and allowing your partner some personal discretion and leeway?

3. Have you already noticed that you and your new partner have different patterns and habits when it comes to spending money? What do you like about your partner's style? What don't you like? Rather than fighting and bickering about money, are you prepared

to learn from the perspective and values of your partner, perhaps even changing your own behavior?

Every once in a while, a frugal person remarries a frugal person. These two will probably inherit the earth—or at least manage a lot of its rental properties! Every once in a while, a big spender remarries a big spender. The result is likely to be scorched plastic (credit cards) and an overall financial meltdown. More typically, one partner is more "spendy" than the other. One partner is the thrifty one, the bargain hunter, the one who worries more about money and spending. The key is to learn from each other, adapt to each other, and control your natural tendencies.

4. Who carries the checkbook in your remarriage family? Many couples retain independent checkbooks and bank accounts for a while, even though they also set up a joint account. This helps each person continue their previous patterns and practices; it avoids "asking for permission" before spending some money. Other couples pool their resources right from the start. What seems best to you?

Few things in life make you feel more successful than managing money wisely. Even if it's not a part of your past patterns, make it a part of your present reality.

DISCUSSION GUIDE
CHAPTER TWELVE

Break Out the Crazy Glue

1. If you have experienced the loss of a marriage partner, did you discover that this loss served to strengthen your attachment to your kids? If so, your experience is typical of early twenty-first-century

Western culture. In the midst of so many marriages breaking apart, parenting is becoming the new "permanent" in people's private worlds.

If you have children, do you consider yourself a permanent part of their lives? Did your commitment to your children outlast the previous marriage? Does it seem, at least in some ways, to be a deeper commitment than your previous marriage was? How do you see this affecting your remarriage?

2. Experts vary in giving advice to remarried persons. "Love the partner more; the marriage is paramount," say some. "Love the kids more; they're yours forever," argue others. How does it seem to you?

Is it really necessary to worry about whether you love your new partner more or less than you love your kids? Perhaps what is needed is to keep on loving your kids as strongly as you do now— but add into that love an equally strong commitment to your new partner.

3. Are both you and your partner working? Do you have children who are adolescents, already busy with sports, activities, and youth group at church? Have you tried to establish some regular "family time" in the midst of your busy schedules? What can you do to carve out "family time" in the middle of your hectic reality?

Attachment to each other, affection for each other, loyalty and commitment—these values are the product of shared experiences. Being intentional about creating these experiences helps you build the family you hope for.

4. With the family as a high priority, you needn't feel guilty about "couple time." Are you establishing time for the two of you to get away, get acquainted, and form a lifelong connection that is nour-

ishing and refreshing to both of you? What specific ideas can you come up with to help make this possible?

Look for help at church, among relatives and friends, and at work. Trade off child care with other couples that are establishing the same priorities. A little extra duty from time to time may make it possible for that romantic getaway to actually happen.

5. It's possible to change your children's thoughts and views about marriage by modeling for them a remarriage that functions well and is reasonably healthy. Both experts and remarried couples say "yes!" to this.

What are your ideas about creating this kind of atmosphere in your new family?

Are you planning for this remarriage to "go the distance" and last forever? Be direct, candid, and consistent in speaking like that, especially around your kids. Help them adjust to a new reality. Do you love your new partner? Show it—in front of the children.

Only time, and God's grace, can move your children's perspective to a new paradigm: that this current marriage is a good and safe place. Your efforts need not be perfect—just persistent.

Recommended Reading and Resources

Selected Books on Topics Related to Remarriage

Adkins, Kay. *I'm Not Your Kid: A Christian's Guide to a Healthy Stepfamily.* Grand Rapids, Michigan: Baker Books, 2004.

Broersma, Margaret. *Daily Reflections for Stepparents: Living and Loving in a New Family.* Grand Rapids, Michigan: Kregel Publishing, 2003.

Chapman, Gary. *Five Signs of a Functional Family.* Chicago: Northfield Publishing, 1997.

Deal, Ron L. *The Smart Stepfamily: Seven Steps to a Healthy Home.* Minneapolis, Minnesota: Bethany House, 2002.

Frisbie, David and Lisa. *Happily Remarried: Making Decisions Together, Blending Families Successfully, Building a Love That Will Last.* Eugene, Oregon: Harvest House Publishers, 2005.

Gillespie, Natalie Nichols. *The Stepfamily Survival Guide.* Grand Rapids, Michigan: Revell Company, 2004.

Lauer, Robert and Jeanette. *Becoming Family: How to Build a Stepfamily That Really Works.* Minneapolis, Minnesota: Augsburg, 1999.

Parrott, Les and Leslie. *Saving Your Second Marriage Before It Starts.* Grand Rapids, Michigan: Zondervan, 2001.

Smalley, Gary. *The DNA of Relationships.* Carol Stream, Illinois: Tyndale Publishers, 2004.

Wheat, Ed, and Gloria Oakes Perkins. *Love Life for Every Married Couple.* Grand Rapids, Michigan: Zondervan, 1980.

Organizations and Resources

Association of Marriage and Family Ministries

Primarily a network of speakers, writers, and counselors working in issues related to marriage and family. Their Web site provides links to many helpful resources; this organization also sponsors an annual conference for workers in family ministry.

Web address: www.amfmonline.com

Center for Marriage and Family Studies

A ministry of speaking, teaching, training, and writing centered in three primary tracks: 1) Marriage renewal and enrichment; 2) Postdivorce remarriage and blended-family issues; and 3) strengthening and supporting clergy marriages.

Directors: Dr. David Frisbie and Lisa Frisbie

Web address: www.MarriageStudies.com

Crown Financial Ministries

Teaching, training, and numerous resources in Christian financial principles, helping families and others manage financial resources according to biblical wisdom and prudent stewardship. Among founders: the late Larry Burkett.

Web address: www.crown.org

Family Life

Speaking, teaching, and special events for couples and families from a Christian perspective, including conferences and seminars. Schedule of upcoming programs and events listed on Web site. Among principals: Dennis Rainey.

Web address: www.familylife.com

Focus on the Family

A global ministry organization devoted to strengthening the family through broadcasting, publishing, speaking, and equipping. Produces and publishes numerous resources for many aspects of family life; some materials are available at no cost upon inquiry. Many other resources available for purchase or as gifts with donation to the ongoing ministry. Founder: Dr. James Dobson.

Web address: www.family.org

Getting Remarried

A wealth of helpful information related to the preparation and planning of a remarriage, as well as helping remarried couples with all aspects of family life.

Web address: www.gettingremarried.com

InStep Ministries

Programs, resources, and support for single, divorced, and remarried persons from a Christian perspective. Focus on reconciliation, restoration, healing, and hope. Directors: Jeff and Judi Parziale.

Web address: www.instepministries.com

Institute for Family Research and Education

Resources and materials for families, including blended families and remarriages. Directors: Dr. Donald Partridge and Jenetha Partridge.

Web address: www.ifre.org

Ronald Blue & Company

Christian financial-management services. Focus on biblical principles and effective stewardship from a Christian perspective. Founder: Ron Blue.

Web address: www.ronblue.com

Smalley Relationship Center

Teaching, speaking, and publishing resources for couples and families. Books, conferences, events at locations nationwide. Founder: Dr. Gary Smalley.

Web address: www.dnaofrelationships.com

Stepfamily Association of America

Publishes *Your Stepfamily* magazine. Provides education and support for persons in stepfamilies and for professionals in family therapy. Numerous helpful resources and programs, many with local availability and access.

Web address: www.saafamilies.org

Successful Stepfamilies

Teaching, training, speaking, and publishing materials for stepfamilies providing wisdom from a caring Christian perspective. Conferences at various locations. Numerous helpful links to other related organizations on the Web site. President: Ron L. Deal.

Web address: www.SuccessfulStepfamilies.com

National Association of Social Workers

The National Association of Social Workers maintains a network of social service providers in each state, organized through its state chapters. By making contact with the chapter in your state, you can obtain information about providers of counseling and other social services in your city or region.

The NASW Web site maintains a database of information, services, resources, and members that can guide you to locally available providers.

Web address: www.naswdc.org

Information regarding the address and phone number of each state chapter is listed below in alphabetical order.

Alabama
2921 Marty Lane #G
Montgomery, AL 36116
(334) 288-2633

Alaska
4220 Resurrection Drive
Anchorage, AK 99504
(907) 332-6279

Arizona
610 W. Broadway #116
Tempe, AZ 85282
(480) 968-4595

Arkansas
1123 S. University, Suite 1010
Little Rock, AR 72204
(501) 663-0658

California
1016 23rd Street
Sacramento, CA 95816
(916) 442-4565

Colorado
6000 E. Evans, Building 1, Suite 121
Denver, CO 80222
(303) 753-8890

Connecticut
2139 Silas Deane Highway, Suite 205
Rocky Hill, CT 06067
(860) 257-8066

Delaware
3301 Green Street
Claymont, DE 19703
(302) 792-0356

Florida
345 S. Magnolia Drive, Suite 14B
Tallahassee, FL 32301
(850) 224-2400

Georgia
3070 Presidential Drive, Suite 226
Atlanta, GA 30340
(770) 234-0567

Hawaii
680 Iwilei Road, Suite 665
Honolulu, HI 96817
(808) 521-1787

Idaho
PO Box 7393
Boise, ID 83707
(208) 343-2752

Illinois
180 N. Michigan Avenue, Suite 400
Chicago, IL 60601
(312) 236-8308

Indiana
1100 W. 42nd Street, Suite 375
Indianapolis, IN 46208
(317) 923-9878

Iowa
4211 Grand Avenue, Level 3
Des Moines, IA 50312
(515) 277-1117

Kansas
Jayhawk Towers
700 SW Jackson Street, Suite 801
Topeka, KS 66603-3740
(785) 354-4804

Kentucky
310 St. Clair Street, Suite 104
Frankfort, KY 40601
(270) 223-0245

Louisiana
700 N. 10th Street, Suite 200
Baton Rouge, LA 70802
(225) 346-5035

Maine
222 Water Street
Hallowell, ME 04347
(207) 622-7592

Maryland
5710 Executive Drive
Baltimore, MD 21228
(410) 788-1066

Massachusetts
14 Beacon Street, Suite 409
Boston, MA 02108-3741
(617) 227-9635

Michigan
741 N. Cedar Street, Suite 100
Lansing, MI 48906
(517) 487-1548

Minnesota
1885 W. University Avenue, Suite 340
St. Paul, MN 55104
(651) 293-1935

Mississippi
PO Box 4228
Jackson, MS 39216
(601) 981-8359

Missouri
Parkade Center, Suite 138
601 Business Loop 70 West
Columbia, MO 65203
(573) 874-6140

Montana
25 S. Ewing, Suite 406
Helena, MT 59601
(406) 449-6208

Nebraska
PO Box 83732
Lincoln, NE 68501
(402) 477-7344

Nevada
1515 E. Flamingo Road, Suite 158
Las Vegas, NV 89119
(702) 791-5872

New Hampshire
c/o New Hampshire Association of
    the Blind
25 Walker Street
Concord, NH 03301

New Jersey
2 Quarterbridge Plaza
Hamilton, NJ 08619
(609) 584-5686

New Mexico
1503 University Boulevard NE
Albuquerque, NM 87102
(505) 247-2336

New York City Chapter
50 Broadway, 10th Floor
New York, NY 10004
(212) 668-0050

New York State Chapter
188 Washington Avenue
Albany, NY 12210
(518) 463-4741

North Carolina
PO Box 27582
Raleigh, NC 27611-7581
(919) 828-9650

North Dakota
PO Box 1775
Bismarck, ND 58502-1775
(701) 223-4161

Ohio
118 E. Main Street, Suite 3 West
Columbus, OH 43215
(614) 461-4484

Oklahoma
116 East Sheridan, Suite 210
Oklahoma City, OK 73104-2419
(405) 239-7017

Oregon
7688 Southwest Capitol Highway
Portland, OR 97219
(503) 452-8420

Pennsylvania
1337 N. Front Street
Harrisburg, PA 17102
(717) 758-3588

Rhode Island
260 West Exchange Street
Providence, RI 02903
(401) 274-4940

South Carolina
PO Box 5008
Columbia, SC 29250
(803) 256-8406

South Dakota
1000 N. West Avenue #360
Spearfish, SD 57783
(605) 339-9104

Tennessee
1808 W. End Avenue
Nashville, TN 37203
(615) 321-5095

Texas
810 W. 11th Street
Austin, TX 78701
(512) 474-1454

Utah
University of Utah GSSW, Room 229
359 S. 1500 East
Salt Lake City, UT 84112-0260
(800) 888-6279

Vermont
PO Box 1348
Montpelier, VT 05601
(802) 223-1713

Virginia
1506 Staples Mill Road
Richmond, VA 23230
(804) 204-1339

Washington
2366 Eastlake Avenue East, Room 203
Seattle, WA 98102
(206) 322-4344

West Virginia
1608 Virginia Street E.
Charleston, WV 25311
(304) 345-6279

Wisconsin
16 N. Carroll Street, Suite 220
Madison, WI 53703
(608) 257-6334

Wyoming
PO Box 701
Cheyenne, WY 82003
(307) 634-2118

About the Authors

DAVID AND LISA FRISBIE make their home in Southern California. They've been happily married for 27 years and counting!

David's personal ministry of speaking began in October 1973 at a Christian campground in rural Kansas. As an ordained minister, he has conducted and participated in more than 300 wedding services in North America and Europe, usually also conducting premarriage counseling sessions with each couple.

Now frequent speakers at retreats, camps, and seminars, David and Lisa have greeted audiences all over the world since 1982 and are also active in a local community of faith.

And grace happens. In the late 1980s they began working with divorce-recovery groups and seminars for divorced persons. Out of this emerged a ministry to remarried persons; from this ministry emerged the book you are holding.

As executive directors of The Center for Marriage and Family Studies, David and Lisa preside over an ongoing educational resource center aimed at helping marriages and families adapt, adjust, and thrive. The Center is nondenominational; it is also nonpolitical by design. Neither the Center nor its directors endorse candidates for office, comment on legislation, or produce voter guides of any type. (Further information is available at www.MarriageStudies.com.)

- To schedule a presentation or program featuring David or Lisa Frisbie or both, contact:
  > Lisa Douglas
  > mountainmediagroup@yahoo.com

- To reach David and Lisa Frisbie, please use the following e-mail address:
  > Director@MarriageStudies.com

- For information about the Center's resources and programs related to divorce, remarriage, and blended family issues, please contact:
  > HopeFinders@secondbirth.org

More Help for Your Marriage and Family
from Harvest House

Got Teens?: Time-Tested Answers for Mom of Teens and Tweens
Jill Savage and Pam Farrel

Jill Savage, founder of Hearts at Home ministries, and Pam Farrel, cofounder of Masterful Living Ministries, help you with practical, biblical tools to

- identify and develop strengths
- make choices over what kids can do, and who with
- teach manners, compassion, and social responsibility
- guide relationships with the opposite sex
- turn around destructive behavior or bad habits

In this fresh look at parenting, moms will discover how to better face the hardest and most rewarding job of their lives.

Seven Keys to a Healthy Blended Family
Jim Smoke

Bringing two families together to create a new one can be a daunting task. Jim Smoke, bestselling author of *Growing Through Divorce,* offers practical ideas and solid insights to help you handle the changes, enhance communication, deal with children, former spouses, and former in-laws, and address money issues. With insights from parents and children in blended families, it all adds up to a resource full of down-to-earth advice and encouragement for building a positive family life.

Making Life Rich Without Any Money
Phil Callaway

With wisdom and laugh-out-loud wit, Phil Callaway shares stories about people who are rich—in the kind of wealth that has nothing to do with money. The best things in life are not really things, says Phil…and surprisingly, they just may be in your own backyard.

> *"Reading Phil Callaway is like playing in Holy Sand.*
> *You're having so much fun, you don't realize how much has gone*
> *into your shoes and is now sticking to your life."*
> —author Chris Fabry

101 Ways to Romance Your Marriage: Enjoying a Passionate Life Together
Debra White Smith and Daniel Smith

A host of "I love you because" ideas and "how to wow your spouse" dates to help keep your love blazing! Romance author Debra White Smith and her husband, Daniel, bring together ways to create special moments to keep your hearts entwined:

- *Making Your Hero Sizzle* delivers innovative and exciting ways to romance husbands.
- *Making Your Lady Swoon* provides unique and easy-to-do suggestions to charm wives.
- *The Hero and the Lady* offers creative and romantic activities couples can do together.

When Pleasing Others Is Hurting You: Finding God's Patterns for Healthy Relationships
David Hawkins

You want to do the right thing—take care of your family, be a good employee, "be there" for your friends. And you're good at it. Everyone knows they can depend on you—so they do.

But are you really doing what's best for them? And what about you? Are you growing? Are you happy and relaxed? Are you excited about your gifts and your calling, or do you sometimes think...*I don't even know what I want anymore.*

In this engaging and provocative book, psychologist David Hawkins will show you why you feel driven to always do more. You'll see how you can actually lose vital parts of your personality and shortchange God's work in your life. And you'll be inspired to rediscover the person God created you to be.

When Good Kids Make Bad Choices: Help and Hope for Hurting Parents
Elyse Fitzpatrick and Jim Newheiser with Dr. Laura Hendrickson

Three qualified biblical counselors share how hurting parents can deal with the emotional trauma caused by a child who goes astray. A compassionate, practical guide. Includes excellent advice regarding medicines commonly prescribed to problem children.